Not for one, but for all:
the constancy of hope
and
life beyond.

Seven Gates To Freedom
Awareness & Consciousness

By

AYLA HESPERIA

BYZANTIUM THE AMERICAS

Cosmology: philosophical - theological - religious. Spiritual implications:
positive vs. negative. Faith and Science: the human response.

p. 188 (paperback)

NEW BYZANTIUM
Camarillo, CA 93010-1771 U.S.A.
http://www.New-Byzantium.org/

ISBN 979-8-89216-000-1 (Paperback)
    979-8-89216-006-3 (Ebook)
Library of Congress Control No. 2023917741

Printed in the United States of America

Although herein information is based on the author's knowledge and
spiritual experience in an ecclesiastical context, it is not intended to
discourage, negate, or substitute qualified professional service.

Colored illustration of author's reflective vision of *Seven Gates to Freedom* was
commissioned to *Artist Charles F. Miller* in 1962 and remained unpublicized
by the author. All other illustrations and graphics are by the author.

Seven Gates to Freedom

"Since we must go, ... we should at least
know where we're going!"

Table of Contents

Introduction

It was very long in coming when the decision was made to write the book. It all began fifty years ago.

In view of such a lengthy period, it seems reasonable that the content must be of consequence. Yet, the question arises: If such is the importance, what was the reason for the delay? Was it hesitation; doubt; procrastination? Or was it lack of adequate information?

The answer is: No, none of these.

Early on, there was a limited circulation in few select high places of portion of this work by this same author. At the time, said portion was complete in its own right and also became part cause in a legal action against the film makers, author, and publishers of a book for misuse of this author's name and good work. The issue of lack of completion, therefore, is excluded. Furthermore, hesitation, procrastination, and doubt about the validity of the content are all eliminated, considering where the original work was distributed and the acknowledgments that such dissemination received.

The delay was because of a different reason. It was based on the issue of *timing*. Although the early or foundational work was at that time appropriate for distribution, it was made available nonetheless to only a reduced circle of readers. Its scope was defined within certain limits and it was targeted on a specific group rather than the general public. Since then, much has changed in the world; and, not only is it fitting to approach a wider readership, but also to expand the writing in more detail. The reason to widen the readership relates very much to the main thrust of the book. Its theme about the heightening of human consciousness and the need and means to support such a vital development is now current.

The greater part of the book is in dialogue form intended to make it more comprehensible. The approach is a discussion between an adult and a group of three bright youngsters who are well-versed in reasoning and in language skill. This setting has raised the question whether young people can handle the level of discussion featured in the book. The response is: Yes, they can. And, the wiser choice is: The earlier, the better. Language form used is the major consideration. Nevertheless, this question has no pressing relevance to the book's message.

Even for the less persevering or analytical thinker, the book promises a message of lasting impression. It also contains a colorful and imaginative art work that conveys the written message through impression and sentiment. The art supports the book and the book supports the art. The optimum arrangement is to have both works at hand and present in mind. Each item, however, stands alone in the conveyance of the work's principal message.

PART I

CHAPTER I

The Gathering

Setting the Parameters

It was a pleasant summer afternoon, just about the hour when the sun begins to lose its stinging grip on the human flesh. From the sprinklers, the light shower of water gracefully fanning out into millions of misty droplets gave new vigor to the flowers, which for one whole day yearned for the sun's rays for life. The process nearly scorched them and now they welcomed the quenching effect that only water can provide. Just as pleasant, an aroma seeped up into the atmosphere when that cool water hit the warm dried surface of the soil.

The gardener was concerned with his affairs. A father with his daughter and two sons sat at the south end of the garden.

"You promised, father, that today you would tell us about that marvelous event of the two bright star who fell in love with each other" urged the young lady with disbelief in her voice, considering the prospect.

"Yes … and please explain which two stars so I can single them out" remarked the older of the two sons who harbored an enthusiasm and dedicated interest in astronomy beyond his conventional high school curriculum.

The younger son had assumed a thoughtful look. "What do you mean two stars fell in love?" he puzzled ... "And you spoke of them as persons."

"All right, let's put it all together" was the only reasonable compromise. "There were two stars such as were not since the earth came into being. Many stars rose and shone. These two stars rose and then fell. They fell once but they will rise again."

An impatient interruption quickly ensued from our young amateur astronomer, "Where did you read that?"

"I didn't. Some of what I will tell you I read and most I have not, and I seriously doubt that I ever will. What I have not read came to me by intuition; ... but in the end, you'll be the judge of what I'm saying."

"Can you tell us where to find the written information?" searched the younger brother.

"Yes, it is all in your science books and in the theories that science uses. Yet, all too often we must have the courage and vision to go beyond that. We must give a chance to our intuition as well, in order to unveil knowledge that science is unable to confirm or deny."

"Are these stars in our galaxy?" inquired the sister, the eldest of the three who could also boast of an excellent academic record ... "Do you mean they exploded when you say they fell?"

"It's a sort of explosion. Let me put it this way: From the great Source of life came forth bright rays of light that affect the whole universe—all the galaxies. Some rays reach far and others close. Their outer tips express life: the life commencing at the source. These rays are all one but yet apart. Their energy flows forward to the extreme ends as they reach out to assert that which the source is. This outpouring of vital power gathers forcefully at the end of the rays and hurls itself into a ball of energy. The great momentum appears to detach it from the source, though it stays magnetically linked to the source. A star is thus born and it is called a *soul*. It is purity, it is energy; it is wisdom. The activity leaves its residual that is the waste or byproduct of a divine alchemy, which pulsates and hurls outward, not dead but live and in motion. It too remains attached and strives to draw near to the center of light. It is a variant, a remnant of the pure. And it is called *matter*."

"Then, you're telling us that both soul and matter come from the same source?" reasoned the young lady.

"Yes indeed, it is exactly what I'm saying. Remember, however, although both soul and matter stem from the same beginning, they do differ in expression."

The father was concerned that his three youngsters must have a clear understanding of the distinctions he was making. He went further in his explanation. It was crucial. He was aware of the vastness of the subject that lay ahead and also of his own limitations in coping with it—let alone to carry the responsibility of conveying it and still maintaining intact their individual integrity of free judgment. His intent was not to program them, but to incite them into thinking and evaluating.

Despite their prior training and capacity to reason and to analyze, he still remained apprehensive. Yet, abstract reasoning and the ability to articulate concepts was not an untried quality among them. He also reckoned to himself: *If I lose them now, I will confuse them, and that's unacceptable. In addition, they will relegate the whole activity to fantasy and to an unfounded mumbo-jumbo of entertainment and delightful nonsense.*

He resolved: *I must slow down and spoon-feed them the basics. And, with these basics under their belt they will be able to stay on track and later to expand on the premise, albeit on condition of their own acceptance.*

"There goes the thinking spell again" was the remark from his daughter in an affectionate prodding to bring him back in line—a common routine among the children and their mother when he would go off on a meditative state or . . . absent-mindedness during a discussion.

"All right! . . . I was just checking up on you to see if you were all staying alert" was his poorly concocted excuse. A couple of slanted stares upwards with a twist of the lips and a tender clearing of the throat by the threesome marked the reaction to the unlikely response. With this familiar ritual completed, the conversation continued.

"Remember, then, soul and matter come from the same source: they are one creation. But, the characteristics in each are quite different. By the same token, although all souls are one, they too differ from each other. Matter differs in its own realm as well.

5

Certain things attract certain things and repel others. Certain souls attract certain souls and repel others. The fingers of your hand are all fingers; yet, are not alike, and also their function differs. Each soul is an individual and each individual has likes and dislikes and varied tendencies and talents. How else could there be a universe without diversity? If everything were alike, there would be no universe. There would only be one."

"I guess this is why the two stars attracted each other—because they were different?" the youngest remarked in a casual tone; now able to reconcile the issue based on the more rational context.

The Scuttlebutt

The gardener was leaning over the chainlike fence stretching out his neck as though to reach farther into the neighbor's yard. He was attempting to speak to the neighbor without being heard by others.

"They are at it again…amazing youngsters" he said. "They are young but will carry on a meeting with their old man as though they were the three wise men."

He was confirming what the neighbor had known for some time. The latter, a sociology professor at the university, had often witnessed his neighbor's gatherings. More than once he had himself participated in the meetings and was totally convinced, just as the gardener said, that the three youngsters were not ordinary children. He smiled to the gardener and nodded with acquiescence. And, while the latter snipped off the suckers from the plant he was grooming, every now and then he would sneak a look at the foursome. As for the professor, he was secretly pleased with his neighbor's approach in dealing with his children.

Pretty good schooling job he reasoned to himself. *I'll bet you those kids are warming up for the deep thoughts. What an arrangement. He first relaxes them by making them feel their age. Then, he zeroes in on them. The guy is smart. He should come out where I am to work with the rest of us and maybe teach us a thing or two. Those kids are philosophers… they aren't kids.*

His analysis was pretty accurate. None of what his neighbor did was random or wasteful. It all had purpose. Call it an experiment or call it an inspiration. The fact is that it worked. The father's approach was direct without delays. He was convinced his children would be better off maturing with an objective view of life. He did not deprive them of their age; yet, cognition and reality would have a part. Fantasies were made known for what they are—make-believe to please and to relax the mind. However, when it came down to where it counts, even fantasies had real substance: they were translated into constructive imagination. Santa Claus had been as entertaining for the children as for all others in their early years; but in full knowledge of what he was and what he was not.

Small wonder then, that the professor admired his neighbor's methods and his youngsters.

Thoughts such as the above were not exclusive to the professor. The gardener too, as mentioned, reasoned much the same way. They both agreed about the three siblings. Both were tuned in at that level of reflection where all reasonable, normal persons think alike: When it comes to the real values in life, gardeners and professors are on an even keel. The same measuring stick applies to all, whether young or old, smart or dull, poor or rich, male or female. The worth that was being measured was that of real life, not one that comes from a social, economic, or educational vantage point. The plain fact here was that the three children were stripping themselves of prejudices and fixed concepts and in a progressive and tactful manner they were being introduced into the cauldron of comprehensive and unfettered reasoning. Their courage was also being nourished to become self-sustained human beings relative to practical life and not as dependent wards leaning on the frailties of others. They faced their creative source objectively knowing that they are multiple expressions of one. The nature of their talks with their father was spiritual and they were prepared for the leap. Intellectuality served only as a stepping stone—a trigger to get started. It was a metaphysical engagement conducted without the ceremonial. And it is this experience that both the gardener and the professor admired and respected in secret.

There were others who knew about the father and his children. In addition to the professor and the gardener, four more persons had an intimate understanding of the goings on. This gave a total of six people who would support the father's methods in the hypothetical instance of a social showdown. The quartet itself constituted the seventh opinion. It should not be overlooked, however, that despite their concurrence about the quartet, none of the other six persons lived their lives or believed in an incidental way as the rest or as the father and his children did. In other words, no compulsion existed in which anyone had to agree with everyone else in order for one's appraisal to be considered valid.

Challenge of Novel Thoughts

Whatever was left of the western sky was being scooped up in a hurry by the sun as it readied for its final plunge in the horizon. On the eastern side of the large shady trees the obscurity of nightfall had started its subtle advance. The more eager of the neighboring homemakers were switching on their lights for their own needs and convenience. The twinkle of some caught the father's eye. His youngest son had just conceded to the notion that somehow stars could fall in love. Indeed, as souls they could. But the father knew that more explanations were needed:

"By their falling in love I mean there was an affinity between them. Take, for example, the electric lights you see in the homes on your right. They look alike and in their function blend smoothly with each other. But there is another characteristic that underlies their similarity. They all derive their power from the same source.

"Now, if you compare the lights with some of the other electrical appliances installed in those homes, you will become aware of something else: Lights and appliances both receive their power from the same source; yet, their functions are very dissimilar. The ability of the lights to illuminate and the amount of illumination by each is what makes them different. The two stars we have spoken about, at first sprung from rays of the same source and performed the same function."

"But still, love is an emotion" insisted the daughter.

"Yes, it is. And in like manner emotions have come forth from the original source. The souls we have alluded to have brought forth with them life, wisdom, energy, and the cohesive quality that binds all these together—and which is the emotion that you speak about.

The two stars were separated, but their common qualities drew them ever closer. Distance and time in that unknown environment did not constitute a factor; considering the irresistible attraction for each other that resulted into a union.

"To the life-giving source, the original power, the unrelenting tendency of the two stars to unite was a basis for the fulfillment of another design. This mutual attraction, however, took place prior to the conscious existence of man on earth. And in human terms the event implies inconceivable dimensions of time, size, energy, and persistence.

"Their mutual attraction made them inseparable by any other power, although such conflicts never ceased to plague the two. The net effect was an increased tenacity of the two to favor each other until the practice became an epic reality in the realm of the heavens. This was a case of pure romance based on the unpretentious attraction between two forces that were destined to unite. It may be said, that there never was nor will there ever be a force other than the original source to cause the two souls to drift apart."

"You are thinking of the stars as souls" interrupted the younger of the brothers. His mind always inclined toward logical causes and relationships.

"Yes, I told you this from the start, only that, they are conscious of their existence in a way humans are not aware. By making this point you have touched on that fine difference that distinguishes spiritual consciousness from physical life. You can now see why men cannot be as angels. They simply do not know how, because they are not made to know. And only rarely do they get glimpses of the other life to which they finally return."

"But then, you're also saying that men are, or have been, as angels" appended his daughter.

"It is what I said. And to that I add the same explanation: That, when from the sphere of intelligent consciousness, the souls embark upon terrestrial life, they acquire a new consciousness and become unaware of their previous existence."

"Well, I'll admit that this sheds a new meaning on the world of stars I studied." The older son had fallen into a pensive mood. He seemed almost detached from the group. This was a totally new thought-processing diet he was being asked to digest. The scientific approach had to vanish before his eyes in order to accommodate this line of thinking. True...it was his father speaking and he wished to listen to him faithfully. Yet, he felt that the cost of his loyalty was much too heavy. He had some serious juggling to do with some new and strange values.

He was serene, but his mind was functioning at highest speed in an effort to find an acceptable compromise. He balanced on the thinnest and most fragile thread where falls determine the destiny of many. He would either have to relent and enter into the vast space of spiritual awareness unaffected by the pull of materialism; or he would land on the hard surface of realism where only proof, facts, and irrefutable evidence construe the meaning of life. Then again...he ventured...he may be able to do both.

His inner dilemma was contagious.

A peaceful silence overtook the group. They all shared the pattern of his thoughts. It was a moment of supreme meditation and a quest for achievement.

Then, the daughter spoke: "Are these the first stars ever to be joined?"

"That is also something I cannot know. However, I could lean toward support of the belief that if they were first to transit to the physical world, the event may be appraised as Adam's ultimate union with Eve; followed by the human race as their continuum."

Another silence again befell the group.

Moments later the lull was broken as the father continued: "You must understand that there are stars and there are stars. Not all of them alike. You will remember that, from the original source spring out various expressions of life. The rays shooting forth pure energy give birth to souls, and the residual of this action generates a corresponding energy, which is matter.

"To clarify the subject more, we shall say that both these forms are unveiled to us when we are mentally disposed to accept them. The first, or soul life, we sense spiritually. The second or material life, we experience through our sensory mechanism. We study the first one intuitively by an intangible awareness. Whereas, the second we codify by means of methodical observations and the establishment of the sciences. This total experience unveils to our minds two major divisions of life: the spiritual and the physical.

"These two major divisions or principalities alternately attract and repel each other in times of withdrawal and separation. They attract one another with intensity when meeting with aggressiveness and attack. A continuous pulsation thus pervades the universe and it exists down to the minutest forms of life.

"You see then, the two stars we have been discussing evidently pertain to the spiritual realm of the universe. And, they have made their way through the ages as souls just as the physical stars have done..."

"Therefore, these two stars or souls exist to this day?" concluded the older son.

"Affirmative...We must, however, attempt to discern and also appreciate a pattern of their existence and activity."

Impatience marked the facial expression of the younger son. He had focused on a persistent thought. His eyes glimmered as he asked, "When you talk about souls this way, you mean they are angels?"

"Yes,...again, you may say so."

"What is the difference between men and angels? Men are not physical stars. Are they angels?" The inquisitive mind of the youngster was now relentless.

"First things first" the father insisted. We must first look at the development of the two stars in the great expanses of heaven prior to their conscious life on earth."

The boy interjected, "Do angels live a better life than men do? Why can't men live better?"

The father staged a stoical approach: "Should men look with equal amazement at what angels do, as angels at what men do, life on earth would be better."

Now, the daughter entered the exchange, "How could men appraise that which they themselves do?"

11

With similar stoical poise the father countered, "Men should think as angels do."

These remarks caused a third round of silence.

The father had achieved his objective. His children had escalated to a higher plateau of reflection. They were now relating with the sublime. Earthbound gravity with all its comforts and discomforts was at this point not the only force at play.

This was a metaphysical ingression that permits a sense of physical life. However, the spiritual was the dominant experience in these moments. Effortless silence and tranquility produced a pleasant detachment from the physical world.

Just prior to their meeting they had offered prayer to the Highest for safe stewardship as they were about to embark on their journey: a time when all sensitive channels are open and receptive. The expectation of goodness is primary; yet, caution begs its own place against the hazard of intrusion. What they each saw, felt, and heard is a personal experience, and no conjecture can or should satisfy any extraneous interest. The point is that there was profit in the activity.

Family Anchor and Support

The vastness of the western horizon suggesting the longest mountain range had already concealed the dying glow of the fallen sun. The only hope remaining for a new development was the approaching darkness spreading itself impatiently upon everyone and everything in its endless race with the sun. The family's home was in readiness awaiting the return of its occupants—just like a passenger ship prepared for the arrival of its gleeful passengers. Only, in this instance, the captain alone was the crew: there, shuffling between the kitchen and the dining room, the mother was making ready for the evening meal Her experience had taught her to pace herself. She was ready and willing even to accept an adjustment on the evening's booking. She knew that the meetings could linger for hours. She was not terribly upset, however, aware of the immense benefit the children derived by gathering this way with their father. To her, just as with the father, it seemed that the spiritual nourishment given the children far exceeded the damage a belated meal might cause.

She proceeded to gear her plans to suit the circumstances. Deep in her heart she rejoiced that her children had the opportunity to experience life in its real form, both physically and spiritually. She thought how pleasing this must be to the Creator. And she reasoned: *This must be the church in Philadelphia... Revelation, Chapter 3:8 ...*

> *I know thy works: behold, I have set before thee an open door, and no man can shut it: for thou has a little strength, and has kept my word, and has not denied my name.*

An amazing contradiction: A church so small and frail in physical terms; and yet, so immensely powerful, for she gathers unto herself all of the favor bestowed by her grantor. Clearly, this is the church the Spirit referred to. A family united in thought and feeling. It forms an impregnable core of strength that no devised power can dispel. Economic and political utopias may for a time occupy the minds of men; but none ever did or ever will permanently displace the fundamental stability found in the pure love of a family. Therein is the church the divine Creator acknowledges as His favorite. And to confirm this further, devout teaching compares humanity to a large family whose peace and survival depend on the brotherly love of its members. It is fitting that the name of the most preferred church is *Philadelphia*. It means affinity to brotherhood.

Almost all preparations for dinner were completed. For the loving mother and keeper of the home, it would be more difficult to idle than to be active. And as it is true of all well-adjusted persons— those who have comprehended and have reached peace in life—she found herself content even to tinker with the place settings, plates, silver, and chairs, as though to render what was perfect... more so. It was an outward expression of love for the persons she cherished. A marvel of the universe: such comfort and assurance in doing the finer things in life with ethereal grace and ease. An attribute reserved exclusively to the feminine gender of the cosmos. Then again, why marvel? The whole essence of creation is perfection in the ever imperfect and unfinished world. A challenge was once posed: *All right, since you know, tell us: What is God? ...Define God.* The reply was instant: *Life itself... The Living God!*

13

With serenity such as this prevailing in his household, it is quite clear how the father could devote wholesome and uninterrupted hours with his children. His own tranquility stemmed from the fact that his family's ship was firm at anchor.

A passing look out into the garden through the dining room window convinced the mother that the meeting was still going strong. The view of the motionless state of the sitters informed her that they had all entered into a meditative state, which more often than not was time-consuming. Again, she contemplated the mental and physical discipline the children received was fully worth the price of her patience.

She did not go unrewarded. The doorbell rang. The hour of the day and the day of the week announced the arrival of a frequent visitor. Unless it was a stranger at the door, she felt assured that the dear friend of the family had arrived on her biweekly visit. It made her glad and relaxed. The friend was no stranger, and formalities were not an issue. Her presence was welcome and her company equally pleasant. She was noble and unpretentious. No need would arise to justify the fully set but unoccupied dinner table. Nor would explanations be necessary as to why at this hour the rest of the family was sitting outside in the garden on chairs arranged in a circle. The friend was quite familiar with the habits of the family. She was, however, unique in her own way. The experience the children were registering was not unknown to her. To be more precise, the only reason in her life she did not carry on in a similar way was because of her own choice. She had been well-acquainted with the practice but had slowly slipped away from it since the years of her childhood. This matter concerned her secretly. She was aware of her deviation, but then again, she was pleased. The price she had to pay for following her compulsion was to lose contact with her spiritual self. She had substituted pleasure for commitment. It was easier through the years to let herself go than to sustain a life of constant mental and spiritual regimen. Unlike the children at this moment, she was free to indulge herself in trivial conversation and social amenities. Yet, she knew that all she was doing was to procrastinate. Time when she would have to come to terms with herself seemed always at hand. She knew the showdown was inevitable. Those moments of reflection made her tense and uncomfortable, recognizing that her bewitching freedom was too much for her to resist.

Much as the friend knew about the family, the family also knew about her. The mother had often thought about the friend's attitude. That evening, during a lull in their conversation, the latter fumbled idly through her purse while turning a longing gaze toward the group in the garden. The mother looked at her and thought: *What a pity ... in her heart she wishes for real food, yet she denies her own self. It must be what is described in Revelation.* It was in reference to Chapter 2, verses 1, 4-5:

> *Unto the angel of the church of Ephesus write; ... Nevertheless, I have somewhat again thee, because thou hast left thy first love. Remember therefore from whence thou art fallen, and repent, and do the first works; or else I will come unto thee quickly, and I will remove thy candlestick out of his place, except thou repent.*

Yet, neither did the friend repent nor did she relent, even though aware that some of the sparkle in life was removed from her. She opted to stay as she was—replete with material possessions, personal charm and goodness; yet, devoid of the full measure of life and the contentment of its simplicity.

A few more casual words were exchanged between the mother and her guest. Then, the hostess excused herself and went upstairs to the bedrooms to turn down the beds and to prepare for the family's nightly needs. Her mind was still on her friend. And, as these things frequently happen, one thought triggered the next.

Earlier, her eye had caught the professor at the far end of the garden. She found herself reflecting on him also: *He is different* she told herself. *Now, with him it is all expressed openly. But it's got to be just so. He is meticulous.* She had observed him to be a man of formality and religious protocol. He was an upright, honorable man, and although sensitive, he appeared to achieve atonement only through ceremonial elation. He was a liturgical devotee given to arduous ostentation. His attachment to the ceremonious in religion was so pronounced that it made one wonder whether the liturgical format was a means to his atonement or the atonement itself. It was unclear if he believed in the absolute sacredness of the Eucharistic Host, or whether he thought that the more elaborate the ceremonial the higher the sanctity. Whatever he felt or knew was his own reckoning; except, it did prompt the mother to remember another passage in Revelation 2:12-15 that says:

> *And to the angel of the church in Pergamos write; … thou holdest fast my name … But I have a few things against thee, because thou hast there them that hold the doctrine of Balaam … to eat things sacrificed unto idols … So hast thou also them that hold the doctrine of the Nicolaitanes, which thing I hate.*

The thoughts ran free through her mind. She was amazed to see that sometimes-random reflections such as those she was experiencing are not really random. It seemed they carried with them a tone of authenticity, or at least motive. They appeared to have been flashing into her mind in some sort of sequence. They were random as far as her not planning their presence, but they were also very precise and pertinent in reference to a message being revealed to her. She began to detect a pattern … : *Oh, yes!* How could she have failed to see it? *What I'm getting here is a living confirmation of the meaning in Scripture* she marveled. *Don't you see? Scripture is speaking to me. The seven churches are not buildings and organizations, nor priests, ministers, and congregations. The seven churches are seven different natures and behaviors of man. Why, it's life itself. How didn't I think of this before? Of course, it's the people and the way we live, the way we think. What I was really doing, without knowing or wanting it: I was matching Scripture with situations and people I know. Yes, this is fine, but I must also care not to find quirks and faults with everybody except myself.*

She became deliberate. She tried to look at herself and at others with an objective eye. She came to the inevitable conclusion that deliberately or not she felt her family's approach toward life was the most acceptable one. She sensed that this was not an absolute value, but a relative one. It was relatively better than the attitudes others seemed to have toward life and the unknown. She was concluding this by a simple process of elimination. It was a reasonable attempt, and somehow scientific from her vantage point. After all, she knew life as she knew it. How else could she think? She drew her conclusions from those experiences and people with whom she was familiar. Her approach was quite pragmatic and unaffected.

All of this triggered her to go on. She had discovered a key. Her emotions were not involved. She was looking at things as they are, without bias—or at least without emotional bias. This of course does not mean she was not prejudiced. Her prejudice stemmed from her belief that there is a God. And, unless there was such prejudice, there would be no standard to reflect on people and herself and earning from the experience. Because then, everyone would be faithless and there could be no comparison of differences in people other than their mechanical or functional differences. The great separation that exists among people is their faith or their lack of it. After that, it's just a matter of degree of faith. She reached a conclusion. *This is what the seven churches are about: The people, their faith, and the amount of it.*

Another thought rushed into her mind: *Can you imagine? Oh, this is wonderful! How come I didn't think of this as well? While they are sitting out there, I too am involved here. I'm meditating deeply and didn't even know it. Their benefit is mine too…Hmm…* she paused. Then, her mind slipped to her friend downstairs: *My, my, she is also involved. In her heart of hearts she is linked with us. I'm so thankful she wants to be near.* She leaned against the window frame gently pushing aside the curtain and gazed at the stars with a dreamlike look in her eye. Half her mind was on the stars, projecting her conscious self the full distance away; the other half was cognizant of the glass-pane and the curtain, so tangible and so near to her. She was filled with joy being aware of her dual self: knowing who she really was—half human, half spirit—just the way she was made.

CHAPTER II

A Sublime View

Origin and the Physical World

Outside, the meeting continued. The silence that lasted longer than the previous times was broken with a question from the sister who was gripped in her own self-inquiry and a wish for her father's explanation.

"I do have a question though."

"Yes, what is it?"

"You mentioned before that all stars are not the same...that there are stars and there are stars, as you put it. Then you spoke about the difference in each, as being either spiritual or material. When I first heard it, I thought you meant they vary in kind, but not that they are diverse within their own kind. I then remembered your example about the human hand and fingers."

"You are correct. And the fact of the matter is that both cases apply: There is a difference between the spiritual and the transformed physical state, as well as there is a difference among them within either state."

"And, when does all this separation happen? The youngest inquired—always in quest for a reasonable order in his thought process. He continued, "I mean do these separate types happen together?"

"Sequence is the keyword here. Those that are different before transformation will remain so afterwards. That is, polarity is established in the earlier state, and is expressed later in the physical state. The result, for instance, is the negative and positive, male and female mutual attraction. With the polarity established, the further evolution of energy is manifested in the physical world upon transformation.

"Since life begins in the spiritual realm, as far as your question of concurrence is concerned, it seems reasonable that the polarity would be determined at that stage, and not after the transformation—even if this happens just before transformation. Otherwise stated, it is not the physical world that defines the spiritual world, but the reverse."

"This is quite confusing" our young astronomer interposed. "If we are to think of people as being stars the way we know them in our physical universe; how are we going to speak when referring to people or persons, and to stars, and to souls…it seems all mixed together and not even real?"

"Well, you are right in terms of how people think. In physical terms it is not real, because in physical terms we are constrained as to how we interpret reality. Yet, in our discussion, we have said that physical life is but a perceived outcome of another foundational life, which is the real one. Therefore, to explain all life in terms of an apparent one is not dependable and more than not, it is deceiving.

"This, by the way, isn't to say that current life should not be explored and dominated. Quite to the contrary, life as we know it in this sphere of awareness must and should be studied and explored to the maximum degree possible. All of the sciences both physical and social; mathematics; engineering; medicine; psychology; space; land and sea exploration;…all of it should be studied, investigated, and expanded without limitations. The intelligent understanding of this universe and life in it is part of the code or the key that may inspire how to unlock the gate into the next level of awareness. However, the totality of that effort forms only a part of the larger achievement that is pending.

"Scientific knowledge of the physical world is just that: the world's knowledge of itself. It does not explain the origin of all life. It is only a churning up and the discovery of the workings within its limited self and how it was initiated; but it does nothing whatsoever, nothing to explain how that start came to be and who might have started it.

The Seven Gates

"All told, the course of the great search comprises seven gates to be unlocked and transited in pursuit of fulfillment. Of those seven gates, humanity at its present level has only unlocked the first two gates, which has led to a third Sphere of awareness or consciousness. Each succeeding Sphere envelopes the previous one and supports a form of life unknown and inconceivable in the former Sphere. For this reason, in the ensuing period, humanity must become prepared to transit this level of consciousness and to accept a new heaven unrelated to the present heaven as perceived in all its vastness. This includes any view from any vantage point of the now perceived physical heaven—whether by reason of the earth's axial dislocation, or by migration to other planetary bodies within the galaxy, or even to another galaxy. It can be possible in this context that humanity will experience the unveiling of the new heaven before ever achieving the ability to migrate to other heavenly bodies of the current physical universe.

"No compelling condition exists to believe that there shall be a new heaven only because of an altered view of the same physical heaven from a different vantage point. A new heaven will be of another quality unrelated to the present one. To restate it: to view the same physical heaven from another vantage point is not to look at a new heaven. Passage through a third gate into the next surrounding Sphere of awareness dismisses the notion of sameness and introduces a new sense of being in a new environment.

"It is from the forthcoming environment that energy was projected to life as perceived. Such energy was expressed in the physical world as living beings and as inanimate objects throughout, including the intergalactic world. The force of the human soul transcends that of any sun or planet: the latter being subordinate residuals of the former. Although planetary, astral, even galactic, and possibly intergalactic influences may affect human life; the

21

reverse needs be considered, whereby human mental and emotional force exerts an even more rigorous influence on those objects. Such objects, as residuals, are each connected or assigned and subservient to each soul in some manner unfathomable to the human mind.

"As large as the known and also the unknown physical universe may seem, it is not as large compared to the next Sphere of awareness; not to mention the additional four. The unveiling of the next Sphere will in some manner reveal this.

"Spheres within Spheres, you might imagine, are living fields of energy in constant motion and growth, followed by self-consumption and final decay. They may also be called planets in view of their mobile nature. The Spheres and the process are the perception within the awareness of the human soul. The evolution and enhancement of awareness of the soul leads to the ability of unlocking and entering the gates in sequence, while leaving behind a dissipated Sphere. For this reason, it may be considered that the previous Spheres are consumed as they decay and dissipate but not lost, when the soul progresses; whereas, they continue to exist and function for the soul not yet prepared—which is to say, an event may occur to one or several persons or may be universal.

"Acceptance of and belief in the above notion is by no means a tool to immortality or to biological perfection. It is, however, a positive factor toward the enhancement and retention of vibrant energy and of a refreshed appearance that belies one's age. This is because of the liberating and hopeful perception and expectation of a continued and better life. The human age of fifty in a ninety-year life span is considered to be middle-age. The perception or anticipation of a superior much longer and more joyful life span makes a fifty-year-old feel, act and believe to be very young. All of us in our heart, of course, accept this notion and may even practice it. And, by the way, it is likely that we will be touching on this subject again later."

The Text Qualified

"All right,…we have covered much ground today. It's time to end our discussion. The next step for you will be to read the work titled, *The Great Age*. You'll read it in manuscript form. There is a copy here in my files that you will need to share and use in your own discussions. It's the basis of what we've talked about so far; and we'll also use it to continue in our next meeting. I must tell you in advance, however, to be aware of three features in that work. These may seem an error to you or even a form of bad writing. Yet, it is for a reason that the work must remain in its pristine form free of intensive editing.

"One feature is that you will often see words with the first letter capitalized, when this should not be—whether a verb, a pronoun, or some word in mid-sentence, and so forth. The purpose is to convey that the meaning of the word describes or refers to a higher level of life above the physical.

"The other item is the repeated mention of the higher level of life, such as the spiritual and the like, and the regularity with which reference is made to God. This repetition and frequency are a metaphor suggesting the preferred practical application in daily life of the messages conveyed. In other words, the persistent reference to loftier ideas elevates one to a higher consciousness. The acceptance of mention of God is fundamental and conditions the reader to experience an advanced awareness. Call it programming of the mind, if you prefer; yet, it is an investment in attitude for extracting the most from the reading. Your positive approach in coping with the text will help you get the most benefit. In the final analysis, whether you agree or disagree, it is up to you. Stay with the work until you finish it. You will find that as you progress, despite repetitiveness and often convoluted language, the work will absorb you and will leave you impressed with its message. And, if at any point the language is unclear, don't fret over it; unless you are bent on doing so. Just continue reading. A subconscious grasp of the meaning will follow regardless how it registers.

"The third feature that needs to be mentioned and clarified is that the words *man, him, his, he* and the like will be seen throughout the work. They are intended to refer to *mankind* as a whole and must not be construed in any way to imply favor for the male gender. Their usage is a simple and clear matter of expediency, which shall also apply in our discussions. The reason is to abstain from the overworked *he/she* device whose best application may be found in legal and commercial texts.

"Now,…let's break it up and get washed for dinner. Mother has been waiting too long. Make it quick and …"

"Wait, wait" interrupted the older boy, "I've been curious to know something that you've not touched on at all. You seem to have spoken a lot about the nicer things that lie ahead, but nothing about the opposite. Is the source of good things the same as the one for bad things?"

"Yes, that's right" the young lady contributed.

And the youngest also jumped in to add his remark: "In school everybody is talking about bad spirits and about people being possessed.

Is that the opposite from what you've been telling us?"

"Fine! … You've all made a valid point. There will be a moment when the subject will come up. However, I would still like to stay on course as to when that shall be. My preference is to deal with that matter after *The Great Age* has been read. Then, in the process of questions and comments back and forth, that subject will come up. We will be more coordinated in what we are saying to each other and avoid misinterpretations and various misunderstandings.

"So, let's be patient and take things in stride. For now, it's best to bring this to a close and let's go inside. Dinner is waiting!"

Nothing could have been more satisfying and invigorating than the sumptuous meal that followed. At last, the moment had favored the mother who was beaming with happiness, seeing everyone seated at the table ready to say grace and to engage her usual artful culinary creations.

Good cheer, laughter, and joy marked the rest of the evening, with much casual and happy conversation and even a brief walk in the garden and the youngsters being quite active. A few flowers picked at random were given to the friend in exchange for hugs and kisses as she departed. The family returned inside for the close of the day.

PART II

CHAPTER I

The Great Age

Introduction

Nation above nations and God above Nation is Peace on Earth.

The will of man is not the Will of God; and it is given to man that he might will his choice for or against God. The Will of God is God above Nation and Nation above nations—not nations above Nation and Nation above God.

Peace on Earth is the Will of God.

And at the risk of losing His own children, God has given a free will to man that he might choose his own life. For as He Is, He chooses man to be: free and subject to his own choice of life.

The inference of Life does not mount from the earth upwards, but from Heaven to earth. The sparkle of Life is generated in the Center of the Universe that is the Realm of God; and from there the rays of brilliance point outwards unto the far ends. The total of all rays and each ray in itself are of the same substance, for it is all God. There is not a limit to the reach of light, which is all one as it fuses in motion and motionless with itself. The origin of all that exists reaches the end of the Universe that never ends, as there is origin in the end. Thus, God's life Is. The Sun of the Center commands the Suns that rule over the sun and other suns; but, the

Sun of the Center is one with the total substance of all Suns and suns, which is One God. As the earth is part of the end which is the Center, then life on earth is not inferred from the earth, but from the Center which is also the earth. The life of man on earth is as an end the Center, thus man is a Center. And all is God. The Will of God to choose Is the will of man. Yet, man's will is not the Will of God. When man wills to choose God, it is of the Will of God. When man wills to choose evil, it is not of the Will of God. For all is God. To choose evil is not all. For all is God.

When all is one it is harmony. When all is not one it is disharmony. God is all and God is one. God is One and all. God is harmony. When man chooses God, he wills harmony with God. And as God is harmony and man is in harmony with God, man is one with God. Harmony is good and disharmony is bad, for it is not that disharmony is good-or-bad and not both or neither. God is all and God is One. God is One and all. God is harmony. Disharmony is not one, and God is not disharmony. Disharmony is bad and harmony is good. God is harmony and God is good.

The Age of ages, the Age of God is the coming Age that includes all ages—as in the mind of mortal man time was needed that all Age will be known to him. To mortal man the cycle of life must have beginning and an end; for this is the construction of man as he has willed it upon himself. In God, the will of man is free and when he chooses to be as God, all is revealed to him; for, the Will of God Is that man may will as God. But, in this practice, the will of man must be whole and pure as Is the Will of God; for, this Is the Will of God that man may will as God.

Then, when man shall will as God, all will be God and all will be pure and whole as Is God. The lesser will of man is not the Will of God; for, God has Willed that man shall will as God, and pure and whole. The lesser will of man not being the Will of God, will not render the light to man that he might see the Wisdom of God; and the Age of ages in the eyes of man will be an age as any other age with a beginning and an end. But, if man shall will as God, the Age of ages shall be known to him and time shall be no more; for, then all shall be one in man as it Is in God, and there shall be no beginning and no end. The Age of ages is the maximum of all gifts

28

from Heaven to Earth, for in it man will reach the glory to which he is destined. The stubborn will be mellow and the ignorant will be wise, the poor will be rich and the sick will be well, the mean will be good and liars will be honest, the weak will be strong and the unhappy will be happy, the morbid will be jubilant and all will be good, as in God all Is good—for man will be as God, as he will have reached God.

CHAPTER II

Abundant Life

Reaching for God

Man, himself has the ability to achieve the fullness of his destiny. This is to be found in each individual and in collective humanity. Consider that as the Earth vibrates, thus shall it receive. When evil prevails over good, the Age of God is not the age of man. Though, there will be many who reach the Age of God, not all humanity will reach that goal at once. It is the Will of God that all mortal existence shall vibrate as one before the grand revelation of this Age shall be known to all and one on this planet earth. When mortal man and his society learn that the self is lesser than the Self and its surrounding existence, then only shall he receive of the Blessing of God. The road is difficult in achieving the Grace of the Creator, but the reward is great and heals all wounds suffered in reaching the goal. For those who stay behind it is always a running thought and an inner wish to suffer the consequences only to reach the goal of Grace. To those who reach the goal of Grace, it is never a running thought or inner wish to return to a previous state, even if there are no consequences to be suffered. It is the Will of God that all Creation shall move in the direction to meet Him. But, as the will of God allows man the choice of how he functions during his mortal life, the time of man's decision to will his meeting with God depends upon man himself. In God, all functions of Creation as well as time are timeless, for He has conceived all that Exists. But, in man's perception, all functions are timely, and the privilege of timelessness is only given to man when he meets God. This very burden of time is the suffering of mankind, because man does not resolve to submit to God and thus meet Him. For the wise there is not ignorance that causes fear and anticipation. The burden of waiting does not subdue the wise. To them, there is perception of events to come and the preparation to meet them. For the ignorant there is much fear, as life becomes a battlefield of unanswered questions and doubts that generate fear To them, time is a gigantic factor that multiplies before their very eyes, as the seconds develop into minutes, the minutes into hours, the hours into days, the days into weeks, the weeks into months, and the months into years. The questions that were to be answered in future time, are often left unanswered and are lost in time past, while new and cumbersome questions appear that must be answered in future time again. To perceive all that Is is the Blessing of God upon man; but only if man will relinquish himself to the Might of his Creator. To submit to God is to accept His Power and to solicit It even at one's own earthly sacrifice. Then, the payment shall be great. In the ultimate understanding, man will realize that by sacrificing the mortal self, he has released his self of the weight of ignorance and has gained a better gift in return—he has received the Wisdom of God.

The span of mortal life is a test that man has caused upon himself. In his choice of submitting to God or to himself, he selected the latter; and the very thing that he attracted is to test him for his wisdom. For man to free the Self from the self he must choose to be as God and then all will be as God around him. The decision to choose God is not for the future, for if so it is not of God. God is timeless, and to choose Him is now; when one thinks of time extended, one thinks not of God but of the self. To postpone one's decision is to choose one's self above God. He who chooses God has as of that moment stripped the Self of the self and is marching on the path of destiny. The intensity with which one seeks to meet God determines the velocity towards one's success. This experience may be instantaneous or of a lengthy nature. The wisdom with which man desires the Will of God is the speed of his success. The higher the caliber of wisdom the less is the time involved, and in reverse.

The Notion of Time

As God Is all, God Is both time and timelessness. But, as man-of-time does not comprehend timelessness and timelessness is only of God, time does not comprehend timelessness and timelessness is only of God, God is timelessness above time. For man who accepts God and recognizes Him, he has accepted timelessness and recognized it, as also he has become as God. Man does not comprehend timelessness, because occurrences in terms of man happen in time and not in timelessness. However, timelessness comprehends time because occurrences in the terms of timelessness happen in timelessness and also in man's time; for, in the terms of man all occurrences happen in time. As God Is all and He Is time and timelessness, God comprehends time. As man's concept of time defines no timelessness but only time, time does not comprehend timelessness; for, time is time and not timelessness. But, as timelessness is not of man but of God alone, in that mortal man lives with time, only God comprehends timelessness. Thus, God comprehends time and timelessness, and man only comprehends time. The man who seeks and meets God, will comprehend both time and timelessness. God conceives of timelessness only to distinguish from man's time. Man's assumption of time is not based on timelessness, for he would have accepted and practiced the latter, being the simpler of the two. The burden of time is man's creation, and he must suffer to dismiss it.

Mind, Heart, and Soul

The greatest trial of man is man's own mind. Man learns all aspects of the manifest world wherein his mortal body lives through the function of the mind. The meeting place of the Realm of God and that of man is in man's mind. And, though all Is God, and the realm of man is God, often the mind of man does not perceive this truth. It is not God Who does not perceive man, but man who does not perceive God. In the Age of ages, the coming Age of God upon earth, the curtain of ignorance that veils man's mind and blinds his sight to God shall be attempted open, and for those who see through the truth shall be revealed. This is God's Blessing upon man, and man's blessing upon himself. In the time of man and in past ages, many have been the indications of God that He Is always Present with man. The failing of man to see these signs has been the cause of his continued ignorance to the fact of all Life—God over all.

The Soul of man, to which stage he arrives upon departure from this frame of life, is the element in man that is closest to his Creator. This element is man in his eternal form even during his mortal existence. The passing of man from temporal life is not the end of all Life, but only the end of temporal life. The passing of man from mortality is the awakening of his consciousness to immortality. The practice of life in immortality while in the earthly body is the ability of man to meet his Creator by motivation of his own will, which he has received from God. The Soul of man is eternal and dwells in the mortal frame of man during his terrestrial life.

The perception of the Soul of man is made possible through man's heart; and the knowledge of this perception is made possible by the use of the mind. The mind knows what the heart feels and the heart feels what the mind knows. When the heart feels the Soul, the mind will know the Soul. But first, must the mind accept the Soul, that the heart may feel the mind. When the heart will feel that the mind accepts the Soul; then shall the heart feel the Soul and the mind will know the Soul; for, the mind knows what the heart feels. The wisdom of the Soul is not measured by the knowledge of the mind, for the wisdom of the Soul is not as of the mind. The Soul has created the mind and has thus accepted it. Yet, the mind does not always accept the Soul. Of the two, the wisdom of the mind is the lesser, for the wisdom of the Soul is of God.

The burdens of the mind are burdens of the Soul. The Soul is of God; the Soul created the mind; thus, the Soul suffers the burdens of the mind. The greatest of burdens to the mind is time. What the burdens are to the Soul are ignored by the mind; but the knowledge of the Soul to the mind is not a burden but a relief. When the mind releases itself of its burdens, it then becomes as the Soul. But the Soul suffers by the weight of the mind; and the Soul will be free of the weight of the mind, when the mind accepts and knows the Soul. Thus, the mind will be as the Soul and all will be as one. It Is God's great creation, that God knows the Soul that knows the mind. The state of the Soul is recorded in the heart of man and not in his mind. Yet, the mind will know that there is a Soul. The manifest world of mortality is no more when man is released of his earthly form. The mind is no longer burdened with time and the lesser complexities of temporal life; thus, its consciousness is carried into the realm of the Soul, where they fuse together to become as one. The Soul awakens and releases itself of the burden of the mortal mind. It is a great achievement for those of mortal men who in the life on earth release their Soul from the weight of the mind and from the burden of time. They then become as God and to them the Wisdom of all Creation is revealed. They dwell on mortal earth as other men in the eyes of man, but in their Soul consciousness they are as God. Greater is their gift when their Soul relinquishes the earth-mind in permanent recognition of the true nature of their consciousness, and when they transcend into the Life of the Soul. Then, they are filled with wisdom from Heaven and not from earth; and the choice is theirs to favor a temporal life, that they may be further alerted to the nature of their Soul. But, for those whose mind has not accepted the greatness of the Soul let God be their salvation; for, even as their Soul accepts release from the weight of their temporal mind, much is its suffering as the traces of the mortal burdens stay deep in their higher consciousness. Eternal bliss of an elevated consciousness is the worthiest gift given by God to any Soul as much as maximum suffering is to the Soul that bends under the weight of ignorance from fallacies of its own creation.

Limits of the Mind

Wisdom of the mortal mind is worthy in its own realm—it meets the Wisdom of God and then it desists. The Soul of man is of God, and as it recognizes itself it ceases to use the mind of man. The wisdom of the Soul follows the Wisdom of God, and it perceives the wisdom of the mind. Thus, in its realm, the Soul does not need the mind. The more the wisdom of the mind, the greater is the speed with which the Soul is recognized. The greater the intelligence of the mind, the more conscious is the Soul of the knowledge of the mind. But a mind of great knowledge and no wisdom is not the mind that will accept the Soul.

The wisdom of the mind can teach knowledge to the mind, but the knowledge of the mind will not teach wisdom. A mind of wisdom is unlimited, but a mind of knowledge is limited. The knowledge of the mind comes from the realm of the mind, and it will not accept knowledge unknown; for, knowledge to the mind is what is known. The wisdom of the mind will accept that which is not known; the knowledge of this wisdom permits the mind to probe into the unknown until it becomes with knowledge. It is not man who will discover and explain God, for man is of God, and not God. The wisdom of the mind is given from the Soul by a grant of God. The knowledge of this wisdom guides man into knowing of his Soul, which is of God and knows God. The knowledge of the mind is not the Soul but of the wisdom of the Soul; for, the mind that knows the Soul, is not of man but of the wisdom of the Soul. The knowledge of man is not his wisdom, but the knowledge of his mind. The knowledge of the mind does not perceive that which is not revealed to man by the wisdom of his mind.

Conscious Awareness

Man is conscious of his being upon this planet through the center of mortal body in the area of the stomach. Consciousness may be interpreted by the feelings in his heart and the intelligence of his mind. The consciousness of the center is not of man when the mind is not in tune; and neither is man complete when the heart does not feel; for the mind does not record the feelings of the center. When man is not complete, the consciousness of his being is not upon the earth, but in the realm of the Soul. There is no way for man to live in the stage of earth and dwell in the consciousness

36

of the Soul in one concurrent time without the Will of God. For man to will this gift to satisfy his whim is not the Will of God: as, man must will as God Wills and seek his gift from God. And being that it all is God and God is One and all, it then will be that man shall have the gift from God to be as man and be as God, all in concurrent time.

The mind of man conceives that which is of man; and when he conceives that which is of the Soul, then man dwells in the realm of the Soul were the affairs of mortal man are not affairs of the Soul. To achieve abounding knowledge is not to be as the Soul. The knowledge of the mind explains and predicts that which pertains to mortal man and not to the immortal Soul. The knowing of the Soul explains and predicts that which pertains to mortal man as well as to its own. The knowledge of man's mortal mind is not the key to life, for what is life is of the Soul and knowledge is its child. To ponder life with knowledge, to solve it with man's mind, is how to seek to touch the Soul and deem it not Divine. The key to life comes from above, a gift to all mankind, and not from man's skilled knowledge but wisdom of his mind. For, that which man's mind knows on earth during his mortal strife is given by the Soul from God to man as wisdom in his life. The thought of man can never prove the Soul it seeks to find, for such a Soul is not of thought but of the wisdom of the mind. The thoughts of touch, of taste and sight, what man can smell or hear, are things of life on mortal earth to which all men adhere. For curious man who strives to prove and seeks to know his kind, will only know that which is his within his mortal mind.

Creative Gift

Through his path in life man has learned of the things of God not by power of his knowledge but by the Will of God. In the passing of earth time and during the ages of man, the heart of man has softened and his mind has accepted the truth. This attitude in man opened the way to wisdom that God could come to him. That which was unknown to man became known to him by power of that wisdom. As he accepted the possibility of the existence of things beyond his own knowledge, he became more courageous in striving to obtain these things and to make them a part of his life.

The fact that these unknown things were conceived in the mind of man, were by virtue of these thoughts things for man to have. But, their generation in the mind of man was not a product of the knowledge of their existence, as in the experience of man such things were not existent. Things unknown that take form in the mind of man are things of God and of the Soul, which are due to be for man. The wisdom that controls the mortal life of man is the power that reveals to him the things that man must know.

As in the life on earth the tools of man are servants to his mind, so it is in God that certain men are tools to Him who serve Him in their time.

In the Great Age of ages, the will of man shall not dictate to God, for when He so decides, even the tools of man that he has used shall serve the Will of God. To know of things of mortal life, the things of man's design, is not to know the will of God and that which is Divine. The knowledge of the earthly things is given as a sign, for man to know and seek to find the things that are Divine. The tools of man and mortal man are instruments of time, which he created in his mind to prove he is divine. But God alone controls the truth of all that is Divine, a truth to which the man of earth will in the end resign. Divine is that which God controls, a Wisdom of His own, His very Self, the things He does, which are to man unknown. The thoughts of life that are to man the products of his mind and all the things that God controls are all affairs Divine.

But what the mortal mind perceives is only part of all, a worthy gift from God to man, who answers to his call. It is not man who will decide when God and he shall meet, for only God can render man the power of this feat. The things that men contrive and trust are objects of deceit; they are created in their minds and leave them incomplete. Let God above explore the Souls that dwell in inner men, and then all men shall know of God and life that has no end. Amen.

CHAPTER III

Reaching Beyond

Divine Assistance and Faith

In his search for mortal knowledge, man shall achieve great results, for this is the Will of God. How man uses the power of his knowledge is subject to the will of man: for God has so Willed it in man. The things of life on mortal earth that are revealed to man in his mind are things for man given to him by God, and each time new revelations come to man, it is not that man is as God, but that God endows man. The knowledge of man may be very great or small, but to know God is not dependent upon this knowledge. The Power of God and the ability of man to know of God and to know God are free from any relation of the extent of man's knowledge. What God gives to man in the form of mortal knowledge enhances the condition of man in terms of his self and not in comparison to God. Infinite knowledge held by man will not answer to him the question of what is Life, This is the most exalted secret of all Creation, held in security under the guard of its Only Possessor. To probe into man's environment in order to unveil what is Divine is not compatible. For, that which is Divine is what man does not know, even if man discovers the origin of physical life. The tools with which man probes will reveal to him knowledge attainable by such tools. But even these tools are products of his limited mortal knowledge. When man will know the origin of his terrestrial life, he will know of things unknown to him today but within the bounds of his own realm.

To know the origin of known life is not to know Life, for it is that Life has no origin; and, that which originates is relative and comparable to the existent. The aspiration of man to know his mortal origin will be fulfilled. But, even when this inquiry is answered in man's mind, another question shall arise as to the consciousness of his existence within his own realm. Great discoveries of the terrestrial nature of man and his surrounding environment are the rightful inheritance of man. The maximum of his knowledge, however, will never surpass the maximum of his mortal existence, because the maximum of his mortal existence does not contain knowledge superior to itself.

Man must seek to find the things of mortal life within his mortal limits and leave the things of God to God. To probe into the environment that is not related to the knowledge of man, is to confuse man in his understanding of his own realm. The knowledge of God comes to man when he relinquishes himself to God and with great humility admits his inability to master God. Even of earthly knowledge this is true, when man entrusts his very life to the wisdom of physical laws that uphold him during his life on earth. These laws are in time being revealed to man not by his own knowledge but by the Power of God. Divine Wisdom decides what man shall know. Revelations come from God to man in trust that man shall use the knowledge to improve upon his mortal trial. When man abuses this gift, the result is his own confusion and self-destruction. For centuries and throughout the great cycles of earth time, the revelations of knowledge to man have contributed to his understanding of his own life. The masses of all people are sprinkled with outstanding knowledge about their life on earth, and thus not only the few derive from the Wisdom of Creation. The dynamic power of this knowledge reaching far unto the corners of the earth constitutes a force that determines the shape of its destiny.

The fallacy of man's action does not lie in his ability and desire to inquire about his environment, but in his inability and ignorance to apply his knowledge toward what pleases God. As much as man places trust in the physical laws that govern his earthly life, so must he entrust the Will of God to guide him in the proper use of his earth knowledge. For, man's maximum knowledge of all mortal creation without his patient and humble submission to the Will of God to guide him in the use of his knowledge defines his own destruction. The ability of man to accommodate himself within his temporal environment, cognizant or not of this quality within his self is the basis of his living existence upon earth. This ability in man is a factor inspired in him by the Power of God. It is known as Faith and it explains mortal life when maximum knowledge of mortal life is not present in the mind of man. In similar form, it is required that man shall maintain unbending Faith in the Wisdom of God: even if man possesses the maximum of mortal knowledge.

Faith maintains man in proper balance of understanding of his maximum knowledge and enables greater revelations by God of the secrets of Life. The total ability of all mortal humanity to attain maximum knowledge of its own nature and to achieve absolute Faith in the Wisdom of God pleases God. This collective accomplishment does not preclude each individual to develop one's self into this state of consciousness. And further, at no time shall there be any obstacle to prevent the Wisdom of God to Will upon man the Wisdom of all Life.

The discoveries of man in relation to his environment are not designed to reveal to him the answer to Life, but rather to enhance his knowledge of the intricacies of the mortal universe. It is an endless world to the mind of man, which knows less than the total configuration. Maximum knowledge can be achieved by man at the Will of the Creator; and then his mind shall know the origin that creates life. Previous to the maximum knowledge as Willed by God, the mind of man wanders in endless manufacture of form combinations of the substance of life, which do not lead him to the knowledge of the origin of life. Only the Will of God permits man the benefit of new revelations and his advancement toward attainment of maximum knowledge. But, even when man attains maximum knowledge, the test upon him continues. It is his choice to submit to God and know Him, or to destroy himself. Submission with humility to the Power of God is the key that opens the door to pure Faith.

With the tool of Faith, man secures the opportunity to receive maximum knowledge and thence to know God. To have Faith that man shall receive knowledge is more valuable than for man to assert such knowledge. It is even important for man to know how to evaluate his ignorance. To say that one does not know is an assertion of knowledge, for man knows less than what he believes he does not know.

Coping with Ignorance

The admission of ignorance is on the basis of what man knows, and his conception of lack of knowledge is patented after his knowledge, which in itself is limited. The extent of man's ignorance depends on his knowledge, in the same strength as the extent of his knowledge depends on his ignorance. The intensity with which man accepts his ignorance relates to the greatness of his knowledge. To limit man's conception of ignorance is to limit his knowledge; for, as man conceives the depth of his ignorance, he asserts knowledge and thus closes his mind to further learning. The insatiable desire of man to know does not in fact diminish his ignorance, but to the contrary increases it. Each time that man strives to know, he admits his ignorance. To know all about the physical life of man by maximum knowledge, which contains even the knowledge of the origin of temporal life, does not free man's mind of the question of what is that which gives origin to the origin of life.

Man's maximum knowledge of physical life is but a segment of the knowledge of all that God holds for man. The ever-unanswered questions in the mind of man are only answered by Divine Wisdom that chooses or not to enlighten certain or all men. The physical laws that man does not know or understand, he trusts in Faith. When they are revealed to him, he masters them and continues in Faith. The great Wisdom of God is Law upon the Universe, which man trusts in Faith. And even when man proclaims himself enemy to such Law, he still depends on It in Faith for life, that he can make such claim.

The Matter of Faith

In obligation to himself by the Will of God, man is on earth to master himself and the great Laws that govern him. When man accomplishes this, he receives the permission to transcend into a realm of life that was unknown to him before. To motivate man's life on Earth when knowledge of the controlling laws does not exist in his mind, a Force of God upholds man in place of knowledge. This Force is Faith, a word man made to mean what God bestows in man and beast.

The Power of Faith is that element in man that maintains him in life, after man has admitted his inability. When in expounding his theories and he cannot prove them, man resorts to Faith in order to accept the life he lives. Faith is ever-present in man, for whether he expounds unproven theories or makes no such effort; he relies on Faith to remain alive. It is often the case that man relies on man for the life he lives and still finds it difficult to admit his Faith in God. Even if Faith in God is inconspicuous in all Creation, it should be borne by man in open acceptance, for more gifts may come to him. To fear this Truth is not to fear God, because man who fears God knows that what he thinks God knows, and such a man has Faith in God. It is then, that this fear is of himself and others with him. But man, who fears himself and others with him, who finds it hard to claim his Faith in God, has placed man and himself above God. Man, in his earthly life either places his trust in himself, another man, or God for the sake of that life. If it is not a trust in God or by a grant of God that this will be, this trust has no value. The final decision of God is what will determine the destiny of man, and it is reasonable for man to place his Faith in the Ultimate prevailing power that has control over him. To trust in other men who have no control over one's life, any more than one has control over one's own life, is a false trust that bears no value. To have Faith in God is to repose in that Power that controls all Life. A man can trust others and himself, if first he trusts God. Then, all is left in the Power of God, and others as well as he shall remain in balance with the Law that governs all Life.

Man must let the Divine strength fill his mind with the true evaluation of life and the Force that motivates it. The Great Book of Life is not written by the hand of man, but by God through man. For man who seeks the answer to Life, it will not be found in other men, but within him who seeks. The aiding tools of others often may direct the seeker to the proper road, just as they may usher him to the wrong one. The answer then lies within man himself to seek and choose the right approach that will guide him to what he is seeking. The great prophets of all time are not final in their given word to those who did not believe in them: They warned; for, they were not prophets to the unbeliever. Those who believed had the knowledge. The answer always lies within the seeker and comes in different forms to each individual. The Father God offers His Wisdom and man must accept it. For those who seek the answer, it is there.

For those who do not seek, there is never a question. The offerings of God to man are endless and they are designed to help man of all times and at any time. What was God in a previous cycle of life for some, was useless to others; and, with the passage of earth time, what was useless to some men before, has become as a gift to others in the future. Perfection of Life does not lie in man but in God. The work of man is to seek it out and choose to follow it until he is as God, pure and perfect. In the Age of ages, the Great Age of God, the door is ajar for man to enter. The limit is not of God but of man. For those who see, the road is clear; and for those who do not see, more time on earth must be used. The advancement of man is his privilege; and so is his delay. To lag behind is the choice of the fool; for, the wise will harbor thoughts of purity and perfection far beyond the comprehension of the indolent. And what is new to some men will be known to those who have moved ahead and who look down upon ignorance. The universe of man is the element of life that limits man's mind to the things of mortal sight. The knowledge of man always perceives this fact, these levels of thought must be known to man that he might be master of himself. To measure life as man measures is not to measure Life as God measures. The size of the Universe is too large for man of mortal knowledge to know; and, to hope to know God. For, even if the maximum of all knowledge is as a tool to man, the knowledge of God still remains in God. The span of life from earth to Heaven is immense, as the Great Spheres envelop earth and the signs that neighbor earth. In this frame of life, the things that man knows and the things that he shall know by reason of his mortal faculties and the tools that they design, are all things of mortal life and of the second and third Spheres in the overall formation of the seven Great Spheres.

The large spans of distance that separate the earth from other bodies in the heaven are but oceans of space as those of water that man knows on earth. To travel the oceans of earth does not solve the question of Life, and neither is the question answered by piercing into space. The basic fact remains that man is subject to the Will of God; and in his choice of thoughts on earth, thus shall he receive. To learn of things on earth and all that is around it is the destiny of man; but his greatest victory shall be when he subjects his knowledge, not to his will alone, but to his will under the Will of God. The revelation of the Truth of Life is left to God, and man can receive it—whether or not he knows about his mortal life. In either case, man must always maintain humility before God, for it is little he knows of the great wisdom that can come to him. And, if it is much that he knows, he may lose it.

Shortfall of Knowledge, and Time

To build immense knowledge of the physical nature of man's universe does not secure the revelation of the Cause of life, as life is not its own cause and to know it in detail does not explain its existence. But, as God is the Creator of all Life and of the life of man, He has bestowed upon man the power of his own physical improvement under the same will that governs man to choose or not to choose God. The Faith man places in the physical laws of his mortal nature, transforms into knowledge that he uses to improve himself and his surroundings. By the motion of the bodies in heaven, man has devised methods to measure time. If the substance in heaven, including earth, were to remain motionless in space, and man as related to his environment ceased to move by this reason, time would not be. The laws of nature would not prevail as they do now, and time would not be measured as it is now by motion.

But it is, that in the mind of man motion prevails and thus time is measured. Time and motion are related, and by physical observation man constructs a pattern of thought that can either explain time by reason of motion, or motion by reason of time. In the course of such motion of the bodies in heaven, time is registered in the terms of mortal man, whether or not he is conscious of this. The perception of either of these two elements marks the existence of the other, whether man is aware of it in full, in part or at all. The cycles of little time make up the cycles of much time, as the small motions make up the large motions. The lesser amounts of time are registered in the consciousness of man with more acceptance than are the larger amounts; the same as the lesser motions of the perceivable things are registered with greater ease than the motions of the non-perceivable things. Physical life itself as a vibrant creation is more understood by man in the present state than in the past or future. But both these outer extremes are very present, although the perceiving mind of man does not register their existence with the same intensity as he does with immediate experiences. The effects of the outer fringes of what refers to the perceptivity of man's mind are much related to man's current environment and have an inalienable influence upon his mortal life from the coarser sense of touch to the finer of thought. His actions and reactions are by this fact related to the total condition of all the forces known to him within the bounds of the first, second and third Spheres.

The forces of nature that are physical laws, man must trust in Faith, if he is unable to understand them and master them. Otherwise, to the contrary, he is not adapted to his environment, and he shall either lose the balance of his mortal mind in relation to that environment, or he shall perish in the flesh. The ability with which man is able to conform himself to the acceptance of this Truth and resolve to become the controller of his own fate, determines the shape of his life in the physical state.

The patterns of laws that formulate temporal life may be altered even to the advantage of man, if this undertaking is conceived in the best interest of all humanity. The thoughts of man having their origin in the mind of man are created as small factors by the great forces that penetrate and transcend the entire mortal universe.

Similar to these forces, the thoughts of man from their embryonic state flow out into the universal world of man free of any hindrance and traveling with great speed; and they cover vast distances in space fulfilling their cycle of physical origin and end. These thoughts compounded with thought actions of the past form the thought pattern of the future and thus the life of man itself. The immensity of thought matter registered in space is not perceived by the mind of man in its total form, as he can only grasp that which is related to his immediate experiences.

Thoughts, whether the products of a sizeable community or of only one individual, plunge out into the world and in their path, attract to their core matter compatible to their own nature. The result is the attainment of vast dimensions of the power of these thoughts, because of the vastness of the physical universe surrounding them. The ability of man to avert inflictions upon his kind depends on his capacity to generate thoughts favorable to himself. This capacity on occasion may be found in individuals who are strong enough to influence the form of events by powerful and intense thoughts that affect and save the masses. But most desirable is the collective will of the masses to wish to generate thoughts that shall act in their benefit. Individuals who are prepared and able to avert any harmful thought reaction befalling their community are able with greater certainty to save their own selves. Thus, it is far more preferable for an entire community to reach the desirable state of preparation, whereby they can act to the mutual advantage of each other and of the whole. The lack of unity of effort results in weakness of some individuals and of the whole. That which is good is harmony, and the result of a harmonious effort is good. That which is evil is disharmony and its result is evil. Disharmony is disconnection and disintegration. If the thoughts of man are not in harmony, the reactions that befall him are evil; and compounded by the motions of the great cycles when completed.

God gives his children the gift of the will in the pattern of His Will, and it is left for them to decide which road they shall follow. If the strength of evil in terms of sheer volume is larger than that of good, the inevitable reaction Is the destruction of man. If however, the contrary holds true, the Blessings of God are upon earth. Man has by virtue of his past and his present formed the mold of his future. The time is always at hand to alter the course of life, if man is intent in this desire. It is by this strength true whether man desires to alter his fate for the worse or for the better.

Effect of Imperceptible Forces

Forces that are not perceived by man may not in the light of such understanding be assumed as absent, any more than an event in history may be denied while not perceivable in current time. Man, on earth accounts for time with a deeper perception when he relates it to something within his own understanding. He conceives of events as being more realistic when he relates them to the motions of his immediate environment. Asked to conceive of things occurring in the far past or future and which do not bear a relationship to his actual surroundings, he dismisses the thought on the grounds that such is too remote for his present concern. Nevertheless, in spite of man's reluctance to adapt himself to the understanding of unseen happenings, such do exist and have an immediate bearing on the life of man. As long as man refuses to accept the existence of greater factors and physical influences beyond his immediate life, he subjects himself to ignorance of things that can be known by him. He entrusts his existence to the hands of nature and absolves himself of the responsibility of knowing how to improve his lot. The unseen laws of nature, however, have no preference over any individual or group of individuals. They always work in the prescribed fashion as designed by the Will of God and they forge ahead in the completion of their assigned trajectories. They have a beginning and an end.

Those among men who perceive these laws may at their own discretion circumvent them and even cause others to do so. To know the laws does not mean that they are revealed to be either always desirable or undesirable. They have a function to perform, and they do it. The preparation of man to recognize these laws and to adapt himself to them is the quality in man that places him ahead of or behind his desired advantage. The incessant effort of science to find answers to questions is a praiseworthy attempt as long as such investigation is conducted under humble submission to the Will of God. The falsehood arises when science assumes aloofness and functions on the premise of it being a self-contained sovereign institution of man that will even answer the question concerning God. Science is the finest process of the methodical thought of man. Nonetheless, it is a product of the thought of man; and in spite of its intricacy and forcefulness, it still remains within the bounds of the third Sphere and the mortal capacity of the mental faculties of man. It is the mind of man that created the things that science seeks to explain. And the mind was Created by God.

The knowledge, or its absence, of the fact that unseen influences affect mortal life does not prevent these influences from existing. The past affects the present as the present affects the future in a manifest expression of the motion of all substance in space. The cycles of these motions have been recorded with alert attention in what refers to the more obvious activities around the earth. Although much has been known about the less conspicuous objects and those which are difficult to perceive, it is not accepted by all men to incorporate the influence of the Universal World as a regulating index of their lives. This influence, however, has never ceased to be present. The same as the varied earth positions influence the sensory pattern of mortal man by reason of their relation to the sun, so do the other movements of the innumerable bodies in space affect the life of man on earth. In passing into the different seasons of the earth year, man is accustomed to accept certain climatic changes that he even predicts with considerable certainty. The almost exact knowledge of seasonal events on his planet induces man to apply himself to certain modes of living in expectation of varied weather conditions, vegetation changes, and even variations in his frame of mind. Recurrence of these events has established a habitual pattern in man during the span of his mortal life. The affairs of life that were on earth before and those that are of the future do not interest man in his current state. Such affairs are much too distant to be of any concern to him in this life. But, little does he realize that the great motions of the universe are very much in progress at the time these disinterested thoughts occur to him. In terms of the earth revolving about the sun, this very day that he reflects upon the subject, the life of past and that ahead is of no concern to him.

He reasons that these thoughts are vague and offer no results. But, if he takes the time to think further, he will astound to find that what he feels now, what was in the past, and what lies ahead are all matters of immediate concern when viewed in the light of the greater cycles of the unseen motions in space.

The present actions of man can well define his future, if not at once, at least within his span of temporal life and in that of his offspring. It is worthy to know that the physical results are as acute when seen in terms of unknown motions and great cycles of time as they are when seen within the normal concepts of motion and time. In the coming of the winter season, man in the cold areas of the earth prepares himself and maintains his life by the use of heavy clothing. The conditions of time and motion have taught man this practice, often at his expense. The primary factor contributing to the benefit of man in this instance is his mental acceptance of certain facts. By acting in a prescribed fashion, he achieved a good result. Had he acted conversely, he would have suffered the consequences. By this fact, man who knows adapts himself to the causal conditions of time and motion of the universal bodies in a way that will be in harmony with their demands. Those causal influences that are of the great cycle type may be also perceived in the mind of man and require a corresponding reaction. Their results may be of the same kind as in the conventional type cycles, or of a rare kind not often experienced on earth. The proper attitude of man in his sensual and mental frame is what keeps him in perfect balance with his environment and the laws of nature.

Broader Horizons

Opening of Spheres

In the Great Age, which is the Age of God upon earth, man shall end the third Sphere of consciousness and initiate his first substantive effort to meet with God. The laws appertaining must be followed and honored or the advancement of man shall be limited. In any of the Spheres where man dwells, these laws are paramount and relative to the development of man; yet, they must always be obeyed by man. The ability of man to perceive these laws lies within himself. Their existence is revealed to him by the Creator in corresponding portions to the preparation of man in his ability to accept them and abide by them. Whether man is ignorant of or ignores these laws is to his own detriment. As the great cycles of universal motion progress, the laws become effective according to these motions. Man, either adapts himself to his environment or remains behind the evolving universe subject to physical purges that will either demolish him or reform him.

To recognize these laws and to assimilate them is the best alternative for man; as it is possible for him to understand them and use them to his advantage, or even to reshape them. The opening of each new age is the same as the opening of each day or each year. The duration of each age depends upon its type in terms of the motions affecting it. The cycles most important to man are those in direct relation to his being. Man, himself, whether dwelling on earth or on other bodies in space, is in constant search of knowledge about that of which he is conscious. When he is able to expand his consciousness to a level where now he is not, he has enriched himself with a broader life. And, as he achieves knowledge of that of which he is conscious: he becomes more intelligent.

The level of his consciousness, and thus the extent of his intelligence, is commensurate with his inherent ability to progress. This ability is produced by the intensity of his will and his willingness to submit in humility to the Power of a Higher Wisdom, the Wisdom of God. To negate the presence of Divine Wisdom is to countermand the Law and thus to place oneself in jeopardy by impeding the course of Creation. The laws that are of nature will not be hindered by the obstinacy of man, unless this is granted by God as a privilege. The cleansing of the mortal attitude is as present as the attitude itself; although not as perceptible by man in its total function. The very life of man in its temporal form is the process through which man goes in order to be cleansed. As man strives for his betterment, he is in that instant attempting to broaden his span of consciousness. The suffering of his mortal life reflects the price he pays in achieving his goal. For every part of his advancement, man must pay the price to reach that level where he would be had he not accepted the fallacy of his present state. The influence of habit is much harder to dispose than it is to accept. Man must suffer the consequence of sacrifice at the rate at which he desires to progress and by the amount of his ignorance. The great steps in science reflect the knowledge of man and the sacrifice he undergoes to reach that knowledge.

The answer to a question is not always contained in one direction. So, it is with man and the supreme question in terms of limited knowledge of the reason for man's Creation. A multitude of approaches lead to the achievement of that most precious quest. Man strives to prove to himself his own existence and achieves many wondrous goals built one upon the other in perfect tune with his scientific approach. As long as this approach is rendered to the

Discretion of God, the discovery of new knowledge increases. But, when the findings of science are used in explaining That which is not next in line according to the rules of scientific investigation, the whole structure of the method is disturbed and collapses either from the top by reason of confusion and incompatible premises that do not offer further knowledge, or from the bottom by reason of previous premises not being capable to support the present confusion.

It is necessary for the scientific approach to maintain a steady stream of integrated continuity regardless of sentiment, and it must evolve by reason. This is known to be time consuming, and it is perpetuated by man as past knowledge is bequeathed to new generations who will use it to create more knowledge. It is set from the start that the scientific approach shall follow this pattern and it must do so regardless if knowledge is derived by other means— albeit from the same Source.

Science and Faith

The tenacity of man to live and his subsequent methods of a systematic recognition of life, all stem from one basic Force that is given from God. Mortal insight into this condition, whether man is aware of it or not, is his Faith. The effort exerted to maintain this Faith is his will; and his attitude as to whether he wishes to make the effort is his willingness. In any of the fields employing the methodology of human reason for the sake of discovering the basis of life, the elements of "willingness," the "will," and "Faith" are present. In those who seek to explain life by reason of temporal knowledge, the element of willingness is stronger than in those who do not seek at all. And in those who transcend the field of temporal knowledge, and who accept it in full and recognize the existence of life by a Higher Power, the elements of the will and Faith are strong. The use of temporal knowledge is not a prerequisite for those who recognize life by will and Faith, as they do not base their wisdom on the products of that wisdom but upon the wisdom itself. One who believes in Faith does not depend on mortal knowledge, though he accepts its existence. In another instance, a blend that consists of dependence on temporal knowledge and on faith would need to be done under a certain condition to achieve the same result. And, there are two incompatible approaches that relate to this:

The one approach stems from the knowledge conceived by man through sensual trial. The other approach is that of the ability of man to receive understanding from the realm of Wisdom, whereby he tends to arrive to the same result as in the first approach. The two approaches are not compatible, because the one pursues the proof of the existence of the second by using only the tools inherent in itself and none of those included in the realm of the object it attempts to prove. The other approach (the spiritual) accepts the existence of that which the first approach (the material) attempts to prove, but does not use any of the tools of the first; for it would indicate employment of the first approach and thus would admit its own denial. The only time the two methods blend in harmony is when the first approach (the material) accepts that the concepts of the second are in fact perceptible by its tools. This state of atonement can be reached either by collective mortal humanity or by individuals alone. Science and religion, when stripped of dogmatic prejudice have a potential to achieve the ultimate goal either for all humanity, if applied with that intent, or for one or more individuals.

The arrival of man at the end of the third Sphere of consciousness, occurring at the opening of the Great Age, is achieved by both approaches; whereby, some succeed long before others by the use of the second method, and others succeed later by the use of the first method, while accepting the premise of the first method. The two previous Spheres of consciousness are always in existence in the wisdom of those who know the third Sphere, as even the future of the third Sphere is in the Wisdom of God.

Progression and the Spheres

The first consciousness of man was limited within the boundaries of his own mortal being—the first Sphere. The influences of life about him were meaningful to him only in their relation to his physical self. The vastness of the earth was not present in his mind, as the distances he traveled were small or large to him not by comparison to the terrain around him but rather by the effects on his body. For a long time, he coped with his body suffering the malice of diseases and pains, until one time he realized that the environment surrounding him had a direct relation to his state of being. When this occurred, it was a revelation to him. A new world opened before his eyes, toward which he had long looked but he had never seen: the physical expanse of the earth environment.

He set out to conquer this new world with new fervor, which marked the beginning of his second state of consciousness—the second Sphere. He was now aware that there were two separate matters in his life, which added responsibilities that brought him new pains along with new enjoyments. This awakening revealed to him that in his previous state he was more ignorant and that now he knew more. The immensity of his new condition, however, did not allow him the opportunity of great imagination, as there was much to do to master this new life. Many years passed as he was later able to measure them, because once again he was awakened to a third form of consciousness as he raised his eyes and looked at the skies that surrounded him. He had entered the third Sphere of consciousness. His preoccupations on earth did not allow him the privilege of investigating in person the form of this new world that appeared before him; yet, the curiosity was generated in his mind, wanting to know more about it in proper time.

The stage was set at last—that is, the stepping stone that one day would lead to the Great Age—and now he discovered that his earth preparation was ample to allow him the luxury of a new life in a new world. By the power of his mind and the reasoning faculty it contains, as given to him by God, he has resolved that there must be ample room in which to wander about in space and that there must also be the possibility of life similar to his on earth. His third step of consciousness is a very bold one compared to the previous state of his being; and, it has never been surpassed before, because he had never aspired to achieve such goals. He is now convinced that there is another world about him that is more real than he had thought it to be. He enters it and derives of the fruit of its beauty and wealth; but, at the same time he discovers new sources of pain and sacrifice. This again preoccupies his mind in terms of greater responsibilities and lengths of time than he had ever experienced. The tension is so great that in spite of his success and ability to accomplish feats of travel never achieved before to the planets and galaxies, he has once again shadowed his mind with the problems of the third Sphere of consciousness and he neglects that still further there is another world awaiting him. He has somehow perceived it, of course, but he has not had the time and mental preparation to enter into yet a fourth Sphere of consciousness: which is the area of supra-space. He feels it is there; but, he has much to do in the third Sphere, putting his current affairs in order before time is left to develop new tools that can carry him into the unknown again.

After prolonged activity and positive effort to adapt himself, he achieves dominance in the third Sphere. Yet, now he senses the fourth stage of consciousness where he discovers that penetration into the Inner Self has no limit. He moves ahead again because his experience has taught him that there is much more ahead than what is left behind. A new beautiful world of the Heaven Sphere of consciousness is revealed to him. This is an area where his wisdom is preferred over his scientific routine. His Faith is greater than the need for tangible proof of the existence of God. The area of blue color where every portion of Life is saturated with intelligence and wisdom is his first step into the portals of the realm of God. In this consciousness, the fourth Sphere, man is more sensitive to the Wisdom of God than to his own contrivances that attempt to prove God. It is man's first emancipation from the carnal self and his introduction into the Life of Wisdom and Faith. This is compared to the entrance into the third Sphere of consciousness, prior to the Great Age of mortal man who for the first time recognizes the immensity of his life beyond the limits of his earth time and the influence of his immediate surroundings. He finds upon entering the fourth Sphere of consciousness that there must be a Supreme Force over him who controls the balance of his existence. The system of scientific approach is still preserved in him, but now he experiences overwhelming conviction of faith in the Higher Power.

In the ensuing fifth Sphere of consciousness, which is the Inner Circle of Life—the purple Sphere—man discovers that while in the Spheres of the Great Age and the blue supra-space, his early feelings were justified and that it was worth the effort and sacrifice to arrive here. He now relieves himself of the burden of doubt and learns that God comes to him without the need for his own reasoning. He enjoys this new world of wisdom that has come to him. But, after having derived of the purity of this life and of the privilege of teaching others, he finds that this state of consciousness is not given for its enjoyment alone but for the reason of it being understood and mastered, as in any of the previous Spheres. This new attitude brings man into a more elevated state of being; and finds himself organizing his new wisdom in a systematic pattern of thoughts, not to Prove God but in humility to improve his self. This discovery is for man the Master Sphere consciousness that clothes him with the purple brilliance of light. Great teaching emanates from this consciousness downward unto the lesser Spheres through the wisdom of the Heaven consciousness.

The Master consciousness is a realm of great responsibility combined with the benefits of wisdom, healing purification, and complete understanding of all thoughts of man. The most important benefit, however, becomes his privilege to enter into the Grace of God, having proven his ability to master his consciousness through purification of healing and being ready to enter in the sixth Sphere. This privilege of Grace is the Will of God that man becomes a Son to Him and he enters into the sixth Sphere: the Christ consciousness of white light of purity that man witnessed in his third Sphere of consciousness on earth, when Christ descended in the form of man as Son of God to minister to him. The blending of man with God comes in the Christ consciousness of Purity and is achieved by the complete devotion of man to the Will of God, regardless of the rigidity of sacrifice required. The Divine Golden Light of the seventh consciousness that humbles the soul and dazzles the eyes is shed upon him to give him Wisdom, Knowledge, and Understanding and the Power of Divine Healing. Six more Spheres follow the seventh Sphere of the Christ-God consciousness in the sacred quest to know God; but are ineffable This is to say, the seven Spheres as one, and together with the ensuing six, comprise the loftier Seven Spheres that follow.

Man, alone does not comprise Creation and neither does the earth nor the universe. All that Exists Is God; as He Is All Existence. Man is of God even when he knows not this Truth. To know God is given to all men and not only to few. Let the mind pierce through the veil of All Existence, and it will single out the things that it is seeking. But, neither shall these things stand out apart from All Creation, as they and other things in one form Life's amalgamation.

Although man is part of All, he may not recognize this; but as his mind assumes control his Inner Life arises. Thus, it is that when man progresses from one Sphere of consciousness into the next, though he is moving away from his own center, he is in Truth approaching the Inner Center of All Life that Is God the Creator. That which is a loss to man is in fact his gain, for when he moves away from his own self, he is forsaking a center of ignorance for a Greater Center that Is of Knowledge and of God, but not of man. Amen.

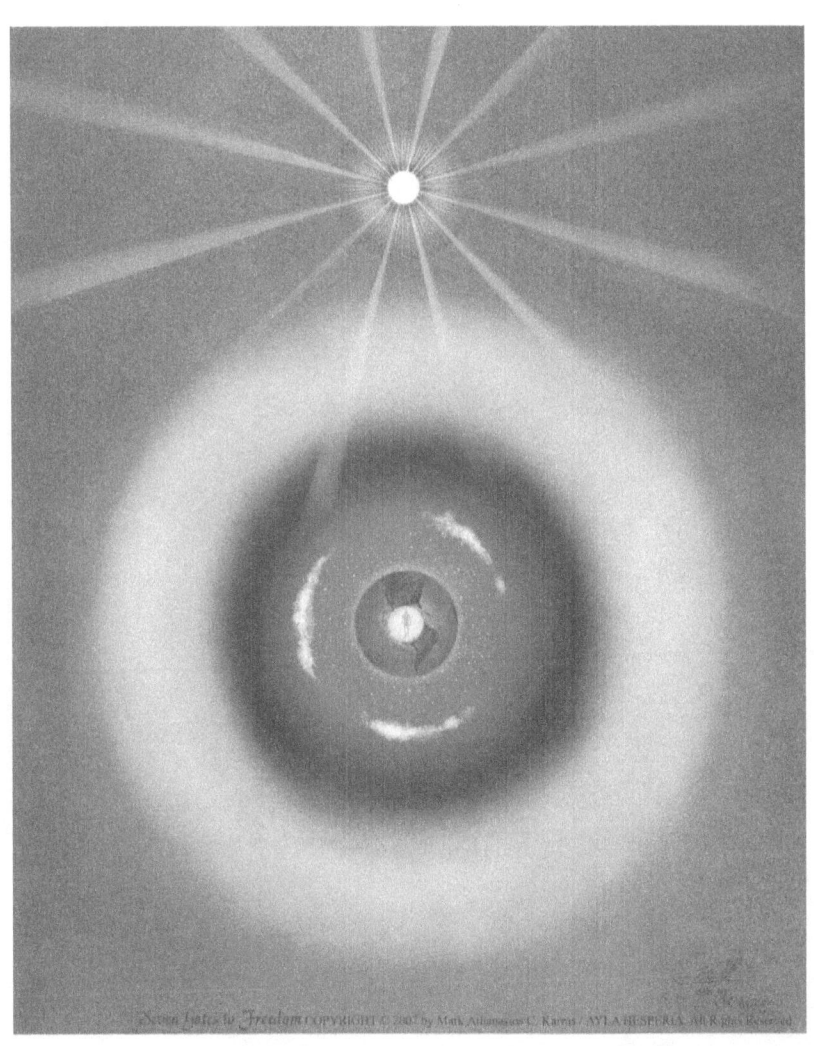

Seven Gates to Freedom

CHAPTER V

Dare to Transit

Sphere Transit and Awareness

For man to know himself is to know others; and to know others, is not unless man knows himself. The development of man is as great as the consciousness in which he dwells. Of what man is aware is the extent of his knowledge; and, he can only measure his knowledge by the things of which he is aware. The time in motion that man perceives in a lesser Sphere of life is as timeless in the higher Sphere. Man, in the higher Sphere knows that the lesser Sphere functions within its own highest limits. That which is measured of the lesser Sphere by the higher Sphere above, is in turn measured by yet another Sphere still higher. Thus, the motions of the lesser Sphere are great to that consciousness, but are small in the ensuing consciousness. As in the case of a laborer who knows only of the daily routine of his work and nothing of the yearly policy of his employing manager, man measures his status only by the things of which he is aware. The spans of time that to one man are great are to the other small; as each measures time in relation to what one knows. To man with the ability to achieve a higher consciousness comes a deeper humility. This gives him the power of self-sacrifice and the vision that he is part of the whole function; which is much greater than the immediate environment of his consciousness. The goal of civilization is the ability of man to subdue his self for the total good; and by his own will and in full without loss of personality submitting to the mandates of All: that is, God.

Past ages and what man envisions in the future are at the time gauged by what man knows. In the third Sphere, the increments of mortal life in the evolution of consciousness are expressed in spans of some twenty-five thousand years from opening to closing of each term; albeit it may occur that not all mortals belong to the same level of consciousness at the same time. The awareness of one consciousness following the other is a blending action rather than an abrupt ending and beginning. Man comprehends this fact when he associates himself with the whole in recognition of a total evolution. The release of the mind from the temporal self as limited by the carnal restrictions reveals to man this reality. Mortal ego is relinquished for the sake of *I am*—in Scriptural Greek, *Ἐγώ εἰμι*—and man attunes with all ages, past, present, and future. Each minor consciousness segment is apportioned in periods of some two thousand years each. As in the case of the transition from one increment to the next, the passing from segment to segment is a blending action that may be marked with some major historical event. Once the ability is achieved for man to assimilate himself with all Creation, the measurement in time of the span of each consciousness is altered in proportion to his ability to assimilate. The entering into a new consciousness higher than the previous one brings with it the ability for man to humble himself and to assimilate with his total environment. Thus, he is able to measure the same trajectory of life in terms different from those he used before. The boundaries of his carnal self are not as prominent in estimating his position, and greater things are shown to him as he has the capacity to absorb them and cope with them.

Since his knowledge is equipped with new methods of understanding, he does not revert to where he was, as he already knows of that life, which no longer serves to please him. That which was measured in terms of twenty-five thousand years is no longer as extensive, for that span of life is lesser in his new understanding and he enters into a higher level of consciousness at a faster rate of speed. Were he to measure it in previous terms of time, he would be consuming every part of that period for moving from one consciousness segment into the next and thus through the Spheres.

The great Universal motions of the whole Creation form the yardstick by which man knows himself. To submit to God is to know all, and thus what is of the past and that which lies in the future by the being of the present. To man shall be known a new dimension that is not of the carnal self and neither of the senses that attach to it, but rather of the mind and of the Soul of man.

From the great Center of Sound to man is given the consciousness of his existence. To limber up the body and let the Power of Life saturate the Soul from the infinite of its center outwards unto the mortal self is the showing of the food of Life that is the Sound of Amen. Thus, God sounds upon His children their Being and all by which It is measured—light, time and motion. In the mind of man, that which is shown in the expression of two dimensions is in one plane, regardless of the suggested design of a fictitious second plane. The character of such design is in reality one plane projected by the mind of man into a second plane that becomes three-dimensional when such other plane is assumed. Comparable to this is the advancement to a fourth dimension that is the plane of Sound—registered throughout the universe but not perceived in the mind of man. The solids are further realized when man senses the influence of the plane of Sound. When this is recognized, the nature of the third dimension to the mind of sound is as the two dimensions are to the mind of solids. The opening into the world of Sound is the acceptance of life before and later and into the present Life as one, as God. Such is the Power to man by God that man shall move into the future and shall know of things that are as yet unknown to him.

Imagination

There is the Life of Soul as life of man is on the earth. To live on Earth is subject to the Life of Soul, as That is under God.

When man achieves the goal of life, he masters what is his, and opens to his mind the door of Soul Life he perceives. No way exists for man to have the knowledge of the Soul, unless he learns by life on earth his purpose and his goal. The way to look into the soul for man is through his mind, to set the way for his reward: salvation of his kind. This way of man through mind to Soul is left for him to find by pure imagination as given to his mind. The work of man in such a case becomes his goal to earn the truth of thoughts and not their faults through power to discern.

That which is imagination in the mind of man must be a positive forward force that leaves nothing free: its action must be bold with the capacity to reach out and to grasp all that it can. The Wisdom of the Spirit is not given to man for the asking, but it must be earned by the complete coordination and devotion of all the faculties of man. The Spirit of man transcends his mortal self, thus for man to reach Spirit he must expose himself to the maximum of mortal sacrifice. The death of mortal man is the relinquishment of his mortal habits and the release of his Soul into Its own realm not hindered by the ties of carnal life. The test is great for man to seek the Power of the Soul while in the mortal self, as he must produce the equivalent of sacrifice of the self to that of its death. This equivalent is measured by each individual in standards of one's own making. For it is, that no two individuals are alike; and, life to each reflects one's own wisdom or ignorance. The intensity of the test relates to the intensity of man's desire to progress. The willingness to subject the self even to its own extinguishment for the sake of God is the most definite way by which man may assure his progress. The rest is left to Him that such a man shall perish or shall live to honor Him on earth. Any selfish purpose for which man shall render his self in part or in full as the object for the attainment of that purpose is deemed by God contrary to His Law: it subjects man to his wish without the benefit of progress. The mind of man places him at the state of being by reason of his current and past knowledge. The actions of man reflect the extent of his knowledge, suffering for what he does not know when ignorance is present. The state of life of present man, on which he has a hold, is life to be that man of God envisioned and foretold. Man's faculty to foresee events by use of his mind, whether such events are foreseen based on previous predictions; or, predicted based on possibilities or probabilities; or, perceived as visions, are all a Gift from Spirit engaging man's mind. The latter of the three is stronger in imagination and in exchange for man's effort and sacrifice in yearning for God.

It is not that man achieves the gift of vision by use of his power to reason: that is, to formulate predictions based on experiences such as in historical conclusions on the basis of intermediate events. The tool of reasoning produces foresight based upon the knowledge of man, much as his reasoning will define acts of history in the light of known occurrences. There are events of life that do not fall within the reasoning knowledge of mortal mind. The study of events, whether through history or science, is subject to interpretations consistent with the knowledge of man. A Power that is greater than man's reason takes place when man achieves knowledge of life beyond the limits of past or present consciousness. This Power is by God to Spirit and to man who harbors Spirit in his heart— known to those around him as imagination. The conclusions of the mind of man based upon the facts of his temporal life are products of his own, which may be true or false. But, attributes of Holy Breath inspired at times unknown are gifts from God to man on earth to learn what is his own. Imagination is a pure concept that must be cherished with care; and, it must never be confused with or assigned to thought that are not of its quality. Man of wisdom distinguishes between his reason and his imagination. What floats adrift unbound by both should not be named as either, for thoughts of mind that have no goal are makings of the idler.

And, neither must man believe that thoughts of value greater than the maximum rational thoughts of man are products of the total or collective mind of mortal man: for, such a total mind will not afford to man knowledge it does not possess. Thus, things unknown to the total mind shall come to man by grace of God. Be it the total mind or the lesser mind, when receiving knowledge beyond, is not accomplished on its own. Neither the total mind nor the lesser mind has the power to give or to receive, unless interceded by another Power above their limit. The total mind of mortal man is not the Mind of God but a created mind limited within the bounds of knowledge of created life. Imagination is the conduit; which, when it is permitted, obtains knowledge beyond the mortal limits. The acquisition of new knowledge enhances the store of mortal knowledge, preparing the way for man to transit the Gates that lead in sequence to the higher Spheres. The ability to know all that lies within the limits of a level of consciousness allows admission into the next level. Of this power is the mind of man, when it receives from Spirit and thus ceases to be of mortal life.

Linking with Spirit

Man connects with Life in Spirit through the medium of his mind. He is conceived and perpetuated on earth by the power of his mind, which is the actual food to nourish him into life. The manifest world of his senses and the needs that they carry with them are products of the mental imagery of man who embarks upon life of his own making and assumption. The major problems of carnal survival on earth are minor contingencies to the Life of Spirit. To master the life on earth, man must first accept the Life of the Soul and the power of the mind as the only means through which he communes with his Self. He must not subject the Soul to a study under the standards of his mortal life, as the latter is but a product of the former. The same as on earth where there are levels of distinction among individuals regarding their general preparation and development, so it is in the Soul Life. The fact that man is on earth attempting to emancipate himself from the fallacy of his assumptions indicates his lack of Soul preparation and his inability to progress into an advanced consciousness. From the great populations of Soul Life in the world of Spirit above mortal life emerge the masses that inhabit the planet earth. Even within the bounds of life on earth marked during the period prior to the opening of the Great Age, man has shown his propensity to elevate himself into a higher consciousness by actions that he took.

The cumbersome years in the early consciousness and man's usage of the natural tools of the earth for his protection and progress were followed by his incessant effort toward another mode of life that brought greater ease and thus also spiritual enrichment. He employed the gifts of the earth in combination with his ability to think; namely, the use of metals, for example, and the power of his mind. The intensity of his thought patterns was commensurate with his activities and the objects he used. This principle of consciousness continued in the ensuing years of his life. The method of his living was always related in a direct manner to the dynamic of his mind. It was never that new materials were made available to him by their sudden appearance before him; but rather, that thoughts occurred to him as to how he could use those materials that did exist in his presence, and which were already within his grasp. God is ever present before man as He Is within him, relying upon the ability of man to recognize this fact.

An extensive use of water was the period to follow the knowledge of metals giving man the opportunity to investigate and conquer the face of the earth he occupied. He had now progressed into a life of fine perceptions, and his preference became to handle those materials that were compatible with the density of his thought patterns. This, being a state of the evolution of the mind, finds man delving in a substance that is by far less dense than any of the materials he had treated before. In this phase of his life on earth, man now copes with the element of space, which in every instance requires his ability to think and conjecture in his new direct experience with what he is treating. The continued effort of man to improve himself will place him in a position whereby his thoughts, as generated by the activity of his mind, will in the ultimate summation of all his knowledge coincide with the elements he manipulates. Thus, the findings of his efforts will be of an intangible nature at the level of his highest thought capacity, not detectable by the mortal senses but rather by the mind. And, in that state, man shall have reached the maximum of his temporal consciousness; being then prepared to enter into the next higher consciousness of Life.

Use of the sensual self will not serve a purpose at that level of being, in as much as it is appropriate only in its own realm.

Matters to be treated ahead are not perceptible by the self, as the latter will have been discarded for having served its usefulness. The equivalent to this phenomenon is the relinquishing of life in the form of death of the mortal self. It appears to man that death of the body is a dramatic occurrence, as all of the aforementioned processes take place within a limited period of time and in comprehensive witness before the unconditioned response of man. In reverse order to all that man attempts to accomplish, man's life is to have received from Life through the function of the mind. To shut off the channel that carries the flow of life from the intelligence of the Soul, is to close the mind in acceptance of life in descent and thus end it.

Next in descending importance for the preservation of life is the cosmic energy derived from the environment surrounding the earth, and following this is the air man breathes; the water he drinks and the food he consumes.

Each of those elements is important to man to a definite degree, and together they represent the pattern of life as derived from the realm of the Soul. In the mind of man, where life is broader than the needs of the carnal self, man can extend that life beyond the span achieved by anyone who limits such life within the bounds afforded by such needs. In times of suffering and want this truth becomes known to man. And, even where humanity has administered relentless hardship upon the minds of men, it is often proven that a stronger Power endows them with deep convictions that maintain them in balance and quite in life. The Life of Soul is free from the needs of man and gives to him the greatest Power upon its first contact with man through the portal of his mind. The density of matter that is needed for man's mortal survival reflects the degree of Soul preparation and attitude toward that survival.

Food is denser than air, and it is the latter that man uses most to live. It is also the latter that is closer to the point of convergence between the maximum concepts of man and the elements that he manipulates in the expression and practice of his life. Let God control the Life of Soul—man's destiny to find: The Will of God and not of man, through practice of his mind.

Life of Mind

That which is man is his thoughts. The conditions of mortal life are the products of the mind of man, as the very life of man is the parent of these conditions. For man to praise God because of life on earth is naught: as God is pleased when man adores all Life. The Truth of life is not of life but of the Life above, Which is the Soul direct from God and thence to man below. Only the preparedness of the Soul merits the favor of advancement in mortal man. Although all men on earth are in life for the same reason; yet, among them there are distinctions that make them different one from the other. It is well for man to know the purpose of his life and of the problems that surround it. The acceptance of existence of his problems, and even suggests the methods by which he can combat them. An attitude of self-assured arrogance toward his life is not practical and instead of solutions it produces further confusion and frustration. The position of the fatalist is only in part correct; and this, because only a part of the total composition of Life is considered. In the eyes of the fatalist certain events are inevitable and bound to occur by predetermination. To a limited extent this doctrine holds true, but only when a portion of the preceding causes and their subsequent effects are viewed. It is thus a belief of partial truth conceived by the mind that tires long before the exhaustive examination of all factors is accomplished.

It is always necessary to apply great analytical efforts to determine all causes and effects in order not to be fatalistic. If the mind that scrutinizes accepts that the reality of events extends beyond the restricted limits of past and future life, it is that such a mind is not subject to the inadequacy of fatalism. The attitude of man is twofold—he is either passive or active. As God has inspired a will in man after the image of His Will, it is the duty of man to exercise this power in willing service to the Giver. The effort to accept even by mental practice the existence of Life beyond the life of man on earth is a positive forward action by man to free himself from ignorance. It is at times difficult to engage in the practice, but that is also the cause of man's indolence and subsequent folly of his acceptance of fatalism. All events of life have a cause and a reason; later, themselves to act as cause in future events. In the strength of man's life on earth by the cause of the past and the effects of the future, he finds himself bound by circumstances he can either overwhelm or to which he becomes subjected. The degree of his ability to overcome these circumstances depends upon the progression of his Soul and his awakened cognizance of that progression. A man whose awareness of this fact is broad is capable of wondrous accomplishments that relate not only to himself but also to his environment. Problems of sickness and other temporal afflictions are mitigated or are almost or fully removed.

For the individual whose mental preparation does not permit acceptance in full, in part, or at all of the principle of Life above the life of man, the ability to control the factors of his life is reduced in proportion to that degree of acceptance. Man's life on earth is not only a pleasure but also a task. To await the occurrence of events is not a sign of action, unless it is the intent of man to foster random events. The error of man is to misunderstand life's design. Once this motive has been established, man must prove it in practice. And, he begins to live his life until he learns that God declares the purpose of his being. The choice to accept random events is the product of man's own design. Yet, even when man acts in error, he receives the Grace of God when he strives to be in tune with all Creation and remains active. To initiate a thought and not to carry it out with courage is the practice of the fatalist and is itself an error—not of the Will of God.

Man's flawed approach to life in arrogance of knowledge, obscures in him the vision: his own soul to acknowledge. The Will of God by that of man when given second place, in fact is First and saves man's Soul through His Forgiving Grace. The fate of man is not his Faith as it is not a Force, it tells the future by the past and present life in course. As such, his fate is false design of life by man on earth: his time of birth, events of life, their form, his time of death. And fate is not his destiny that often man mistakes, for he can change its character by action that he takes. To pray to God and to request the influence of Grace, is first in place to save man's face and him from Soul disgrace. The facts of life are either acts caused by the mind of man, or they are pacts by man to God to serve by His Command. Thus, it is wise for man to seek from God that he be led, that He might rule his fate on earth in life that lies ahead.

The destiny of all existence is one: it is the ultimate assimilation with God. This Force cannot be altered, for it is a Design by God upon His Creation. The fate of man is but a phase attached upon this Force; it takes a shape, propels itself, and comes back with remorse.

Such cycles continue to recur as often as it is necessary until the fate of man is one with the trend of destiny. The fate of nations or individuals is witnessed on the *tree of Life* and it can be studied and evaluated by the Intelligence of God and of Those Who serve Him. The progression of man from one Sphere of consciousness into the next signifies his ability to read and understand the cycles of life that always have and still occur. The more that man is sensitive in life, the better his ability to read the cycles. As man progresses into the higher Spheres, he is able to comprehend not only the meaning of the cycles but also the direction of the trend. His knowledge is thus more complete, and he can understand future events on the basis of past and present occurrences. The Intelligence of the Soul and the Wisdom that man derives from it are similar to man's method in achieving knowledge in the lower Spheres by the process of reason. The difference lies in that the higher consciousness of man derives its Wisdom by considering broader factors of Life that contain life. In his progress, man begins to be more sensitive, and he feels reactions from influences other than those to which he is accustomed. His mind is alerted to new experiences of life by additional dimensions in space. The past, the present and the future become closer, as in his mind he perceives them in actual connection with each other.

Through the medium of his mind man is able to contact the past and the future in one concurrent thought. As his conviction of this notion is increased his receptivity from these areas becomes keener. Man, in this state has greater Faith in the existence of That which he does not know. The result of this experience is a reciprocal reaction on his part and of the areas that he contacts. Once the mental attitude of man is opened to such receptivity and as long as man is willing to continue in its acceptance, the benefit of recognition of the unknown areas becomes subject to his demand. It is to say, that man assimilates with that which lies around him and he can demand its presence the same as it requires his acceptance. This cumulative admission of knowledge is said to be wisdom by those who have not accepted it. In reality, knowledge exists for all men, but not all have accepted its existence. The suffering of mankind and that of individuals is not because it is itself an element in existence as a sovereign body with which man must cope. It is a product of man resulting from his lack of knowledge. This lack of knowledge refers to his inability to perceive all the factors that comprise his life. If man were able to reflect upon his life in relation to knowledge of that which he was and which he will be, he would control his present state.

Functions of Choice

Teachers and Students

In order to achieve the knowledge, man must first accept the Existence of God as his Creator in terms of infinity; a power that never ceases to Exist, as He had never had a start. Man must conceive God to Be a Living Force Who contains all of man's known nature and even aspects not known by him. The principle underlying this precept is the preparation of man to accept even the most remote possibility of the existence of Creation far beyond his own understanding. This attitude enables him to justify the acceptance of any condition of life that he is unable to prove in his current status. It is a method similar to that used by a physical therapist, for example, in the exercise of certain muscles for their restitution; but, in this case the attempt is made upon the mind. Just as the trained muscles will be able to perform remarkable feats, so will the mind of man be able to perceive thoughts that were unknown to it before. The pattern suggested is not a simple one, which can produce results in a limited time span. It is a copious method of learning, which demands many hours of effort and trials of self-sacrifice. This form of learning has been the gift from man to man in space of generations; and it is not the act of physical endurance, as it is of the mind. It is wisdom that comes to man, not by the effort of others but by the will of man who tries and for the sake of God. Many have sought to find a school where they might draw the knowledge, but the system hereby advanced is by the will of man and by his own indulgence. The answer to the question how knowledge can be derived without the use of schooling is that when man submits to God and seeks to find the Truth of Life, he is given all the learning. If time is there that man must be in such a teaching place, there is no reason to despair, for that will be the case. As in any aspect of man's life on earth, so is the measure of teaching proportionate to the desire for learning. It is man himself who decides the nature and amount of teaching that he receives. Otherwise, teaching is not offered free and to the unwilling student. The Wisdom of God is not to be cast away at random that some might gather it and use it. It is the Will of God that all those who seek shall be tested and few shall be chosen. Neither is it reasonable that teachers should teach to the unhearing ears. In all Creation the principle or Life is reciprocity and effects of cause. To minister to the unwilling is to lose one's own knowledge; for, the echo of the voice of wisdom shall be ignorance. It is important for both teacher and student to choose each other: For, as an unwilling student is a detriment to the teacher, so is an unprepared teacher a danger to the student. Only the intelligence of the Soul has the ability to seek out and guide one to the other. Man is what he desires.

It stands then, that the quality of knowledge given to man shall equal his wish. Thus, God comes to man if he will seek Him. Those who teach man are those who seek God; and to obey Him is to serve Him and All He has Created. The price of indolence is ignorance, and Wisdom is given as a reward to him who tries. To try and reach God is not to fail but to succeed. The extent of man's success depends upon his desire to succeed. Many are teachers and many are students. The amount of wisdom treated within the mind of each is produced by what the teacher aspires to teach and that which the student desires to learn. In either case, when the yearning is for God, there are many returns to be had, depending upon the quality and extent of that yearning. There are no schools that bring the Power of the Creator to man: they only point out the way; and it is the self that must do the work. Those of man who receive from

God are teachers to those who seek; as the Wisdom of God is Love for All, which fortifies the weak. Unless man is accomplished as a student in the Learning of Life, he must not assume the role of teacher; except to practice his knowledge in reverence to Principles he is entrusted. Contrary to this rule, it is deemed that such man is not worthy of the confidence vested in him. His practice is to be contained within the bounds of service to others, not in the guise of teaching, but as a silent Praise to God and at his own sacrifice without ostentatious recognition. It is this quality that the student must be able to discern in a person when choosing. He who is of God as His accomplished instrument to serve Him on earth admits the need for further knowledge and seeks it with no rest. It is that even the qualified teacher of the Spirit of man assumes the role of the student and serves with no demand. The greater the development of man, the less is his assumption of All knowledge as it is that the admission of ignorance harbors the seed of learning.

There are limitations to the mortal mind regarding knowledge in the development of a Spiritual seeker. Unlike man's requirement for any teacher of mortal service to know the details of derived knowledge; it is not necessary for the mortal self who serves God to know of such matters—unless this is given as a privilege in return for service. The immensity of knowledge derived from Soul Life is incomprehensible by the mortal mind; and once attained by that mind, it becomes as Soul itself.

Man serves God by his existence. His ultimate return to his Creator is the only course man follows even at his own ignorance. For those who recognize this truth and accept the Power of the Soul, their mortal progress is assured, and they serve as channels through which the Holy Spirit communicates with the life of mortality. This improvement does not ascribe to material gains or pampering of the ego. More often and contrary to this belief, a sacrifice of these desires is required, unless the opposite is decreed. Progression of the carnal self involves preparation of the body and all its associated functions, in order to receive a Soul residence by the Power of the Holy Spirit. The body becomes a servant to God to minister to other men. It is useless to demand progression by mere desire generated in the mind and motivated by the wishes of the mortal ego. For man to seek selfish success in this respect is to demand for his own sake that Holy Power shall dwell within him. In proper form, man must first submit to God and plead for His Decision to permit him the privilege of being His servant. A sincere request of this nature permits man the opportunity to embark upon a trial of learning. The tests that are given are the measure of man's ability to earn his request. The higher the aspiration, the more stringent are the tests. And by trial-and-error man's Soul prepares the self as a pure House of God.

What the mind of man achieves in the field of science by the use of tried mortal knowledge is all known to Spirit by His Wisdom. The tools of man are his servants, as the tool of the Soul is man. It is thus that from the Life of Soul man on earth becomes as an instrument to Spirit. All that man constructs on earth to serve him in his knowledge is placed in man by the art of Spirit to serve Him and mortality. The importance of achieving the position of a Spiritual teacher is great in that it reflects the Soul of man reaching a level of higher understanding; and also in that a developed mortal is an asset to humanity in rendering service to its benefit. To reach fulfillment in the world of Spirit while in the mortal self is above all important, because man becomes ready to advance upon arrival to the Life of Soul. The recurrence of birth is mandatory for man who does not respect this knowledge. Of such man is the mortal world comprised, requiring his presence on earth until he is convinced, he needs not return for he understands the Cosmic Law of God. The Soul of man dictates the nature of the self, and whether on earth or in the Life of Spirit, man shall progress. It is preferable to dwell in the life of mortals in order to cleanse the self of ignorance. The memory of life on earth is carried into the Life of Soul and their man is evaluated. The Life of Soul is not in the conscious memory of man, although on occasion revelations of that Life have been known to man. Often, the privilege of knowing the Life above is granted to man when he is a proven servant of the Law of God.

Service and the Soul

For man to serve God is to be an instrument of honor. To serve any other force is the stagnation of the Soul and the delay of progress. The nature of man whose purpose is service to the Almighty is not different from any other mortal.

There are Powers vested in man, however, which he uses under the direction of God and His Emissaries. The Powers given are beyond the scope of man's maximum knowledge, and They are not rights but privilege. Before man can qualify to attain this honor, great tests are given by God to determine his strength or weakness. The principle of testing is to subject man to hardships that will induce him to invoke assistance. At such times, the weak, attempting to avoid the effort, surrender in defeat and return to ignorance. Whatever their results are, they have violated the Law and they must complete their mission at a later date—probably in life beyond this time. The strong, however, try to maintain themselves in courage and in Faith that these tests are of the Will of God and are designed to save them, and not to destroy them. It is known by the strong that salvation of the carnal self for its sake does not improve the Soul. Thus, they continue in trust that the results of their efforts will in the end determine their worthiness.

This is the man whom God seeks for His servant, and when Power is placed in his hands it shall not be abused. For such a man who shall revert from love for God to evil, the price he pays is even death, his peaceful Soul's upheaval.

Different gifts may apply to different workers who seek to serve as instruments of God. Some carry a combination of several gifts, and others only one. But, whichever the gift upon man, he must serve with diligence. Divine Wisdom is not known to man that he might judge the reason for the gift. In all instances, the nature of the instrument's development is in line with the characteristics of the self and the preparedness of the mind. Much time is devoted by the Intelligence of Spirit at the beginning of development, to determine the best instrumentality suited for the individual.

The time required to develop an instrument is related to the quality of the subject. Some individuals need longer periods of preparation than others. There is also the consideration of the purpose for which the student is being developed. If it happens that a certain instrumentality will serve its use at a much later date during the subject's life, then it may be that such a subject will be completed near the time of the inception of service. Man must thus obey the mandates of Cosmic Law and leave the time of completion and the type of development to the Will of God. To demand a phase and seek to procure it is folly, as this is the product of the mind or man and subject to his will, not the Will of God.

The methods of development are also unknown to man and are in rare instances manifested to the mind of man for his observation. Each Age brings new reasons for the mortal development of servants, which always remain ahead of mortal knowledge; and who might serve others as guiding lights for progress and invention. Although the basis of all knowledge remains the same, the methods of its acquisition vary to suit the prevailing circumstances of life. These circumstances are the product of the attitude of man programmed in his destiny and must be served within their own perspective. The previous purpose of man's development was what it continues to be, and it is identified with ceaseless effort to realize perfection in the mortal world. Above all considerations stands the requisite of perfect discipline in the function of mortal man.

Divine Healing

Health of the body and the mind of man is the phase of development served by Divine Healing. All other considerations of life are subsequent to this most important requirement. In the life of Christ as Jesus upon this earth, it was His Divine ability to Heal that offered the world a most dramatic conviction that in Truth the Power of God Exists.

The eminence of Divine Healing as a phase of human development shall continue to be so until the convergence of man with God: for He Is Divine, He is Perfection, He Is Healing. In the case of mortal instruments endowed with the Power of Healing, the highest or all phases of development are channeled through their bodies. The source of life is from the Soul as granted by the Creator. Life is maintained by methods designed to subsidize it through the use of Cosmic Energy brought before its reach. When the attitude of man is not in balance with this function, the mortal portion of the Soul suffers discrepancies that are manifested in various ways, either through disease, penury, unhappiness, war disagreement, or any of the undesirable conditions of life. The Power of Healing enables direct contact with Divinity and the channeling of Vital Force from the area of Life beyond that of man that brings soothing influence upon adversity and the strength to dissipate it. The equilibrium of life is maintained by the proper intake of Cosmic Energy, and it secures a conditioned order in the affairs of man, much the same as this very principle is apparent to man when he maintains good health by proper breathing and intake of food and water. The Power of Healing cleanses and also reconstitutes the person and enhances the normal flow of Cosmic Energy from the surrounding Universe.

It is essential for the recipient of Divine Healing to accept with confidence the Power of the Healer. Otherwise, the balance of intake is disrupted from flowing forward and makes it difficult for the Healer to function. In many instances, the attitude of man shall heal him without the intervention of the Healing servant, on the basis of his own reopening of the channel of intake of Vital Life. Men who are instruments of God must be revered if not as men but as His servants. The saving of such men is a credit to all those among whom authentic workers may dwell.

Man attempts with care to invent and make tools with which he can communicate, transport himself, and heal. He is cautious to safeguard his tools that they shall not be damaged. It is with equal care that God's instruments must be regarded. The devices man conceives, designs, and makes are to the Intelligence of Spirit already known; and they are placed in chosen individuals who function as instruments of God. The world of Soul is eager to communicate with man, whenever the latter is ready, willing, and prepared to accept.

The substance that comprises man is the same with that which comprises his devices. When man uses his knowledge from God, he can accomplish greater feats than those achieved by physical empirical experience. The preparation of man by Spirit for sending and receiving knowledge to and from Life of a higher consciousness is done by the intelligence of that consciousness and by the patient cooperation and willingness of the subject. The construction of intricate machines designed by the mind of man is but duplication of what is achieved by the Power of Spirit in chosen instruments. Man's trend to fabricate his own devices and to depend upon them for use in higher achievements predicates extensive inventiveness and the use of elaborate machines to accomplish similar goals obtained by gifted mortal instruments. The delays and disappointments are great in the same measure as the size of the aspirations. Although the efforts are made by current generations, the fruits are derived by future ones who rely upon past knowledge. The progress of man relates to the attitude of his mind. The world evolves in the manner that man chooses. No guidance is forthcoming from the world of Soul different from what man invokes. The discovery by the mind of man of Universal Creation is accomplished by the method that best satisfies his inquiry. Man receives that which he seeks. The capacity of his inventiveness is in proportion to his courage and aspiration. No revelation shall be given to man that shall upset the balance of his understanding. Each motion of the Universal World is complete and effective. There is nothing given above what is received. The ability of man to comprehend his nature is only as good as his effort. What man accepts is what he knows. Man of the first Sphere of consciousness can know the third Sphere if he accepts that knowledge. Man can know God if he accepts Him. It is upon these principles that the world of man is built. His suffering is his ignorance of the Universal Law.

The disturbed condition of his mind provokes sentimentality, which has no wisdom. Dependence upon conditions other than those prescribed by the Law is suffering. Ignorance of the Law and to reject it is the plague of mankind. The Wisdom of Life is Exact and does not deviate from the pattern of Cosmic Law. To want for its sake is not of the Law and man must pay the penalty. The desire for God and for His sake is what the Law Commands; then, all that man needs in his life is given in his hands. Man's entire life is judged by the precepts of the Law, and each action of thought he experiences determines his future. There is no personal regard in the execution of these precepts, as only the Will of God prevails over all considerations. It is to man's advantage to abide by the Law in order not to be penalized and thus to lose the chance for progress. The laws of man are of the Law, which gives to man his reason; that he might serve It with great awe lest he be charged with treason. All the affairs of man and the order under which they are practiced are subject to the Spirit of the Law of God.

For any man who assumes the interpretation of man's law over and above the Law of God, the judgment is treason against the trust placed in him. The laws of man are made to regulate his life and not to rule his conscience. Only God reserves the right to that judgment, and it is given to man through wisdom when the need arises and at His Will.

CHAPTER VII

The Real Purpose

Service to God

Service to God is Love for All that God has made. To rule over man without regard of God is to assume that one is greater than one's Creator. The government of man serves its constituents when dedicated to the Will of God and to the precepts of his own law. When man aspires to govern others on the basis of personal gain and for the glory of the self, it is deemed contrary to Universal Law, and he is subject to the penalty thereof. Mortal wisdom must not weaken and bend to the demands of evil, as this is a betrayal of the trust and faith placed upon its power. The guiding Light that must direct all actions of man in the dispensation of his duties for the welfare of humanity is the Wisdom of God given to man through those He chooses. The true man of God knows he is His agent. He who assumes this role at will is dangerous and a spoiler of the abundance of life. Both the governed and the rulers must partake in the equitable formation of government. The Power of guidance given to those who God has chosen as His instruments must be made a part of the life of man both in his laws and in the government that he formulates, assesses, and executes. When man assigns himself the task to govern others in credence of his own ability to rule without the intercession of Divine Power, he is not functioning in the best interest of humanity. The mechanics of government, their precise knowledge, and the ability to manipulate them does not render man the chosen leader and guardian of human welfare but only the agent. Only when man alerts himself to this Truth, shall the world of God be free of the hold of the unscrupulous. The battle is great, but victory is certain, for it is Willed by God that Just Peace shall Rule His World. This knowledge is commonplace to man of Holy Wisdom. Yet, to the mind that has no vision such thinking is unknown.

The ruling of man's affairs is a responsibility of those who govern as also it is a duty to serve those who are governed. The Word of God must now prevail, and Peace must be on earth, as men of Light and those who See shall bring to man his worth.

None of the affairs of life are self-supporting and free from the Influence of Cosmic Law. The entire world of man is a product of Divine Order, which supersedes any law of man. As the knowledge of man is limited to the extent of his consciousness, so are the laws that he forms restricted within the boundaries of that knowledge. No nation shall endure unless it is designed on the basis of reason as established by the requisites of the Law of God. The seed of decay is planted in that people whose government is conceived against the rules of Universal Order. In a global view of what concerns all nations, there shall be no peace on earth until all children of God accept the idea that they must govern themselves in peace. The principle of good against evil applies to nations as it does to man: in that man forms nations. Man's fate in life is what he does and what his mind devises; thus, he must choose the kind of acts and thoughts he patronizes. The system of Cosmic Influence is present around man at all times and it affects him by the actions he takes. Conditions of war on earth are not self-generated but are products of the attitude of man toward his kind. The origin of man's actions is instigated in the mind of man and perpetrated by the power of his will, attracting the corresponding Influences from his original environment. This fact is true in either case, whether man attracts war or peace. These Influences are impersonal and bring to man the result of his desire. The attempt to invoke the

Influence of peace for the sake of revenge is contradictory and shall destroy the pretender.

To interfere with the Order of the Universe is to upset man's own balance. The security of man is at stake when man nourishes evil desires against his kind. Cosmic Influence distinguishes no persons and when summoned it destroys or benefits all things regardless of their nature. The true method of invoking Power from the Universal World is not in how this is accomplished but in what is invoked. Even the slight thoughts of man are instruments of force that drive Cosmic Energy into action.

There is no grace in simple thoughts that mortals always bear, but to achieve the worthy ones is Love for man's welfare. The types of men who dwell on earth are not for man to ponder, as they are there the same as he for God and not his wonder. Let God adjudge why man must live, his frame of mind, his color; and then shall Love prevail on earth and Peace shall claim man's valor. The things that man desires on earth are not always his credit; thus, he must turn to God for help and seek a life of merit. To search for wealth and mortal fame for selfish satisfaction, pollutes the Soul and God-made Law by scorn and by infraction. The wealth of life is not in gain of man's mortal invention; it is in Love for Life and God, for man and for his Nation. The Love of man for other men when formed into one nation can earn in turn the Love of God and procreate a Nation. The Will of God is Peace on earth and Nation over nation, the Love for man, for Cosmic Law, for God of All Creation. This Is the Word of God to man, His Will and His Command; It Is the Sword to Guard His Plan. Amen, Amen, Amen.

PART III

The Next Gathering

Sophistication and Inquiry

This time the quartet met in the den where ease and comfort were available and where the ever-mindful mother had quick access when serving her refreshments and welcome treats. The relaxed and quiet atmosphere helped much to achieve a meditative state and the ability to assimilate information.

Considerable time marked the interval since the last meeting. Few casual exchanges, however, had occurred among the children during that period. The exchanges ranged from comments regarding *The Great Age* to remarks about what had been discussed at the last meeting. The pattern for the current discussion was thus set. In other words, everyone in the group had a fair idea of what the next discussion would include; which was the objective the father had sought when establishing a common ground of communication. He needed to make the session meaningful. The moment was ripe to justify the next discussion.

"Here we are again as we had agreed" was his opening remark.

"I think we should begin with questions you may have about our last discussion or about any other issues that were raised when reading *The Great Age*. Of course, I haven't forgotten your question about the negative or bad influences affecting life. I am sure, however, that all this will come together as we move on with our session. OK then, who goes first?"

As if on cue, the youngest of the three was quick with his inquiry. The thought must have haunted him for some time because the way he phrased his question was assumptive and focused, almost as though the last meeting had not ended and was still going on: "The spheres are eccentric you said. So, one surrounds or encloses the other. Then, how do you transfer from one to the next? Man is flying out in space now. Does that mean that if he travels out far enough, he will cross over into the next wider sphere?"

"Um, good question … if you're thinking of crossing in physical terms. But we're not talking about physical things. Remember, all of what is physical belongs there and stays there. And the better understanding and handling of it is through the development of the sciences. We must respect and promote those sciences, because they improve our physical state. They do not, however, in any direct way increase our spiritual progress.

"I say direct, because in an indirect way they do help elevate the estimation of ourselves, and so they contribute to releasing us from the downward pull of physical confinement."

"Well then, that leaves only the spiritual awareness as the means to realize the transfer" added the sister.

"Yes, you are correct. And it is through our mental faculty that we are able to perceive that principle.

"And not only does the mental faculty provide the means, it is also the speediest of any other methods … if indeed any other methods exist. It is the mind through the faculty of imagination that achieves the result. Not even the speed of light can approach the quickness of the mind; let alone to consider the physical ability to reach another existence or another reality."

"Not simple imagination! … I cannot believe that imagination alone will carry man beyond the universe as we know it" was the skeptical remark of our astronomer aficionado.

"No, you're right" the father agreed. "In fact, to involve oneself in idle imagination is to daydream. And, although such activity may have a certain therapeutic value, it is not the type of approach that reaches the transformation desired.

"And actually, nor is constructive imagination…which is so useful in science…the means by which man shall traverse the spheres."

The look in the faces of the children at that point showed bewilderment. It appeared as though all three were united in one common but inaudible voice, "What are you talking about?"

They had every right. Yet, for the father, it was a moment of opportunity. Their minds and all their senses were wide open to receive any and all information possible. They thirsted for an explanation.

This is an ideal situation, the father thought. He was also comfortable in back of his mind that his children would not accept his remarks without qualification. He knew that first they would engage their judgment and power of discretion. They had been taught well.

He went on: "The imagination I am talking about is not only positive and constructive: it is garnered with a strong sense of empathy. You must be able to live the vision that your imagination has created; and even more than that, you must be able to detach yourself from every aspect of your physical consciousness; and, in your own way, uplift yourself in an authentic and pure manner into a higher sense of being. In other words, you must experience your presence in another level of awareness, which in turn will give you a hint or a sense of recognition of what the next sphere of consciousness reserves for you. It is most important, however, that you must be able and very willing to return to your ordinary state of physical being. Failure to do so, by lack of your will, relegates you to an empty and useless daydream state; or even to hazardous exposure, which we'll discuss in a while. The cardinal rule in all spiritual engagements is the acknowledgement of the priority and sanctity of God. First and foremost, must be a sincere and heartfelt prayer for divine protection. There must be a concurrent positive and unrelenting rejection of all negative. Alertness against deception is paramount. A purchased ticket may get one to a musical concert;

but only authentic prayer and humility opens the way to spiritual growth and enlightenment.

"The inability to achieve this transference is not in some way an infraction or a denial of ultimate success. It is only a phase of development in a continued course of preparation. It is the destiny and right of every human soul to reach that eventual goal.

"Remember also that it is not possible for a mind bent on affairs of physical life even to begin to approach such transformational awareness."

A period of silence and a meditative mood prevailed again. Moments later, one of them mumbled, "And we have four more transfers following this third one ..."

"Yes, we do!"

Then, the sister puzzled: "But, you also said that there were six more spheres after the seven?"

"Right again. And, let me elaborate on that a bit more. Think of it this way: The first seven spheres in themselves comprise one total sphere, which is the first of another set of seven spheres yet to follow. Our colored art depicts the set of seven spheres we have discussed up to now. The six additional spheres are expressed in the white circle centered on the top portion of the art, beaming out the life-giving rays that energize creation.

"It is foolish and hopeless to believe in yet only one life similar to the present one. The human soul thirsts for much more; for in its depth, it is conscious of its far richer heritage. This is why I mentioned earlier that human souls are not victims of the stars but masters. Human souls are the stars."

"It all sounds so pure, so high and so hopeful; ... but isn't it unrealistic compared to what we know? "We must learn to think that way" the sister added, being the eldest and more mature of the three.

"Yes. Then again, isn't it better to see it that way than to live one's life believing it to be expendable, hopeless, and used up? Think about it; ... and, the older one becomes, the more significant that way of thinking is. Does one want to grow old and feel old; or is it better to age while still feeling, acting, and living as a younger person?

"The broader view of life seems to be the choicest way."

The Negative Aspect

Instances of reflection and meditation were frequent during the gatherings as it may well be imagined. These were challenging thoughts that provoked the best of sound judgment and sentiment of even the young siblings. One must not underestimate or be surprised by the capacity of young people to absorb and to appraise ethical, moral, and spiritual issues. It is best, for that matter, to deal with these subjects quite early in life in order to establish the foundation upon which later life evolves. Reshaping tree branches and tree trunks is not easy or even possible after trees reach their maturity.

Refreshments for the group as expected arrived in good time. The moment to serve them was just right. The mother knew well the pulse of the meetings and did not intrude prematurely, causing interruption when the youngsters needed to absorb and evaluate the information received.

Return to casual conversation and body language were the indicators suggesting to the father the time to resume the discourse.

"OK, ... I'll be the one to start off this time. I'm going to take it that your question is still open regarding the negative aspects of what we've discussed so far. Is that all right with you?"

No response came forth. Yet, it was more than evident by the expression in their faces, and even by the echo of their silence, that the three were in full agreement. Indeed, so many nice things had been expressed so far that it seemed quite unrealistic to continue with the same. Besides, life is never so perfect and so straightforward. The credulity of even the very young is put to the test when grownups try to over-exaggerate their point. How much more does this hold true where such new and unknown heavens were expected to be believed by these alert and sophisticated youths?

Nevertheless, the father pressed on. His comfort zone was the caveat he had established with his offspring. He knew they were steadfast on that issue—which in the final analysis allowed them their own discretion whether to accept or to reject what he conveyed.

The project at hand had to be completed. He could not stop at this point. A significant question was still outstanding.

"Let's approach the subject this way: Does a negative force exist as something inanimate—a mere force—or as a living entity?

"Based on our fundamental notion of life projected downward to the physical cosmos from the spiritual realm, the appearance of both positive and negative at the lower three spheres is expected. This is not to say that the negative resides entrenched in prevailing power at the higher spheres. It is conceded, however, that it has a presence in first, second and third level spheres—the known to us physical world. Consider that what may be an acceptable presence at the physical level coincides with the parallel unacceptable presence at that same level.

"In other words, if souls appear on the earth as human beings, it Is expected that misguided souls also avail themselves of the opportunity; albeit perhaps concealed or in a misleading manifestation. This, then, begs the question: Is there a living negative presence on the earth? Yes, there is.

"The reason for the negative presence is to be pondered. The original source caused the physical reality we recognize. The positive and negative emanation forms a distinct polarity that we know as good and bad. The negative can be regarded as a means to serve the honing of the human soul in its quest for ultimate improvement, which may be recognized as salvation.

"Whatever that situation may be, it is not as depicted and as practiced by various charlatans bent on producing sensationalism, confusion, fear, and weakness: all for the abject reason of personal enrichment and false acclaim The ignorance of such perpetrators blinds them to the fact of their ultimate accountability—sooner or later. The infraction committed strikes at the very order set forth by Creation. It is not a matter of play and it is inevitable, having defied the sanctity of that order, that they will suffer the ultimate consequence. There is constancy in the cycle of life. This is an impersonal force that traverses its trajectory in a continuous action of self-purification and self-correction. Nothing is left unattended. The affairs of the Creator are not to be scorned, derided, or abused.

"Must man deal with the negative? ...Yes. He must!

"How this is done and why it is done is of major importance. When done for proper cause, it is a blessing. Otherwise, as explained above, it is punishable: The incidence that on the surface is pretended to be corrected—done in jest—reverses itself and instead strikes back with severity. Intent is quite a serious issue.

"Remember what Jesus said about the *unclean* spirit, as given in Matthew 12:44-45:

> *Then he saith, I will return into my house [that is, into The possessed person] from whence I came out; and when he [the unclean] is come, he findeth it empty, swept, and garnished. Then goeth he, and taketh with himself seven other spirits more wicked than himself, and they enter in and dwell there: and the last state of that man is worse than the first."*

The youngest interrupted: "But there, Jesus is really focusing on the possessed person suffering. Other than the negative activity, he is not talking about the perpetrators that you mentioned."

"Yes, your observation is correct. However, let me alert you to the fact that the violating perpetrator is also exposed to the grip of the unclean. Otherwise, the perpetrator would not have engaged in the wrong activity. You see then how dangerous these involvements become when engaging in them without due regard. And we'll be talking more about awareness and also the unawareness of being under negative influences.

"Meantime, keep in mind again that the person who takes on the task—even with the best of intentions and in good faith—links himself to the circumstances that plague the afflicted individual. You can equate the situation to a healthcare worker, or a doctor, or a chemist, when they enter into a setting affected by impurities. These professionals take every precaution to protect them against danger of contamination prior to being exposed to seen or unseen danger. No less can be expected of a worker in a spiritual setting."

"I see now" responded the youngster.

"Good. Although you have understood my point, let me elaborate further. It is simple just to talk about one's protection in such matters. The reality is, however, that the whole issue is far more complex and demanding. Protection as such is the ultimate precaution the worker takes: it is the conclusion that follows a lengthy and serious preparation prior to actual engagement. And again, another parallel is that of a soldier who just before battle equips himself with all sorts of protective gear, camouflage, communications equipment, and other relevant devices in addition to his weaponry and lengthy training. None of this gear is of much value to him unless he has trained long and hard in the optimum usage of it. The same applies to the healthcare worker, the doctor, the chemist, and not least to the spiritual worker.

"Training in spiritual matters is a very long, arduous, and demanding effort. An authentic worker is not one who attends a seminar, only to obtain a credential. That part is but an orientation and an academic scattering only suggestive of the rigor and depth of preparedness that a person needs. The slightest inaptitude, ignorance, failing in faith, or plain arrogance spells devastation for both the worker and the person presumed to be helped.

"I am only touching the surface of what I am attempting to explain. Mistakes in this area are not mistakes that somehow can be corrected. They are deep-rooted and serious, and most difficult to reverse, if not altogether permanent.

"The essential point is that the moment a worker engages in such activity, an inevitable linkage occurs. There is no reversal, and the issue must run its full course. Only the prepared person exits unscathed. Otherwise, the damage can be in time near or in the far future. A final resolution always takes place. It is best, therefore, to abstain. Pretense and jocularity are the worst option."

The father had just finished talking, when the older son raised his hand thrusting his open palm forward in an attempt to halt the conversation.

"Just a moment, please…I'm a bit unclear now. Only a few moments ago you insisted that man in general must deal with the negative. Yet now you are saying that only people with careful preparation should do this. How can this be?"

"Yes, I did say that…and both statements are correct.

"Now, follow my next statement. I repeat how this is done and why it is done is of cardinal importance. When done in proper form, it is a blessing. Otherwise, it is punishable. So, let's take it from there.

"The premise was that from a higher sphere proceeds life to the physical world. It is ponderous, I said, why both positive and negative are manifested. Nevertheless, ponderous, or not, it is something we need to deal with. And, in dealing with it, there are in essence two approaches: the passive and the aggressive. Between these two and without exception, the entire human race is involved.

"Among the many there are few who are able to cope with the problem in an aggressive manner, which is to say that they are gifted with the aptitude much the same as others are gifted with so many other different talents—singing, painting, mathematics, music, healing, and so forth. It is a calling to which they are drawn by an instinctive urge. The remainder great majority of the population belongs to the passive category, which relieves them of the obligation for aggressive action, but not of the duty in one degree or another of preserving their own integrity. This has much to do with their social behavior, moral and ethical standards, and how each person deals with conscience. You see, the negative presence is extremely subtle, always at play in the effort to debase the individual. The issue then becomes how and for what reason one prepares: Is it passive for the reason of self-defense; or, is it aggressive with intent to help someone else?

"I understand all of this" interrupted the youngest. But I keep thinking of what you said about science earlier at our last meeting."

Science and Spirituality

"All right…what is it that I said about science that makes you think about it?"

"Well, you had mentioned that science is separate from the spiritual. But is there any part that science has in preparing one, even if the person is not gifted?"

"You are raising a very valid point here. My contention is not that science is excluded, but that what is of science is not what is spiritual. Even psychology in its makeup is an upward oriented discipline. It emanates from observations in the physical level and evolves upward to the psychological level. In other words, it is first grounded in the physical world, which in turn triggers its analytical rationale concerning the psychological world. As such, it is founded on scientific grounds and observations and then implemented as an art. Psychotherapy, of course, reveals itself quite overtly in that context. Psychiatry, on the other hand, has direct relationship to medical science.

"Spirituality, however, is of a downward oriented character, abstract and detached from the physical; except when it manifests its influence upon the physical world. Therefore, there is a clear distinction that exists between a trained expert psychologist and an authentic unaffected priest. I would like to read a few lines from a diatribe of mine that I have kept somewhere in my files."

While he said this, he reached over to his filing cabinet and tried to locate the work.

"Oh, here it is! Let me just read some of what I wrote quite a while ago:

If you are confused about a spiritual problem and you go to a priest and he speaks to you in terms of psychology, either he is not a priest or he does not understand his priestly duties. The likelihood is that in his heart of hearts he feels his inaptitude, because he never was convinced that he is a priest.

A priest must speak of Godly things; he must speak of faith, and he must speak of things of the soul. To equate his dedication to that of science, he has ceased to be a priest and he has become a scientist. You have gone to him to seek spiritual help. He must reciprocate with spiritual help. To deal with the subject of the unclean, all the academic achievement in the world is not sufficient to do the job.

The unclean is not impressed with academic degrees. He has devised many of them. Think about this: I refer to the following by Walter A. Cogan in a commentary published in 1961 by Good Counsel Publishing, in which he states that, 'In the Orthodox Eastern Church, the exorcists are not ordained. Anyone lay or cleric, who has the gift, may and does use exorcism. This was the practice of the early church.'

The only scientific involvement that we may concede in the practice of the removal of unclean spirits would be the application of methodology or the classification of observations, so others may study and know—much the same as we are doing now. But I repeat, there is no scientific method that can take the place of the spiritual God-given gift to an individual to remove unclean spirits from another in the name of God. It would not surprise me in the least to know that a scientific person involved in a job to assist a person with a severe negative problem, may himself become affected dangerously without recognizing his problem.

Now, let me not be mistaken: We must acknowledge the achievement of science. We must acknowledge the depth of dedication and sacrifice by the entire medical field over the centuries, their miraculous achievements to date, and the promise that they hold for the future. But this does not preclude the scientist himself being faithful and cognizant that there are problems of hidden nature that science has not yet been able to resolve; and never will be able to resolve; because, as I have stated before these problems reside in an area beyond that which we understand in our material life.

I am not trying to promote a polemic, pitting one against the other in the areas of science and religion. I am pointing out the distinct nature within which these two areas function, and the respect one must hold for the other. That which is a physical problem must be treated scientifically; and that which is a spiritual problem must be treated spiritually.

The father continued: "Well, my writing goes on with other arguments, anecdotes, and examples supporting this position. I will not continue, however. Yet, it is clear that sensationalism, repulsive books and films disparaging the sanctity of spiritual purity constitute a direct effrontery. Retribution is certain for the unfortunate perpetrators of these acts. Remember that response to all such events is never left incomplete.

"There is one more thing that you should know: The term, exorcist, is a derogatory term that dishonors and denigrates the office of priest. Anyone who in arrogance attaches the term to a priest commits an infraction and is relegated to inevitable retribution. The Eastern Orthodox Church is correct not to ordain people on the strength of that exclusive practice. The act of prayer and anointing by the priest is sacramental by virtue of the sanctity of ordination in dispelling unclean intrusion. The priestly act is not a practice of lay routine. The sanctity of the priesthood is reserved as an office in the next domain and must not be defiled. In all cases, divine providence determines where and in whom such work is entrusted and who suffers retribution for offenses. Ordination is not a title but of sanctity. This holds true for the priest as well as for the offender against the priest.

Self Defense

"Inasmuch as our purpose right now is not targeted on training of aggressive type workers, we will focus our attention to what the passive group needs to do to maintain its own safety and security. There is no distinction that renders one group better than the other. Both groups are as they have been created, and both groups are fulfilling the purpose of their existence as mandated by the Creator.

"Again, the road to success in dealing with the negative force is long and demanding. This holds true for both categories and not only for the aggressive type. In the latter case, the experience of the worker may vary from that of the defensive person; although there are certain circumstances common between them. One such circumstance shared by both is the critical issue of awareness. I had alluded to that subject earlier and I had promised that we would discuss it."

"Before you go on ..." the sister inquired, "is it as arduous a task for the passive person as it is for the aggressive worker?"

"I'll put it this way: Is it arduous to go through life breathing; or is it something we do regardless of the effort? If we pause and think about it—except for the demand for air—we would tire very soon contemplating the time and energy, we invest in breathing. But this is not what we do. Instead, we keep on breathing happy and content.

"Likewise, the reality of the negative is as present as our need to breathe; and so is our underlying desire for spiritual, moral, and ethical peace and tranquility. In our life, therefore, are we to consider as arduous our quest for peace and tranquility? You can see how from this viewpoint the answer to your question is: No, it is not arduous for the passive person always to be ready. It would only be arduous if no negative existed, thus forsaking the need always to stay vigilant and prepared.

"Arduous or not, the commitment to watchfulness is for life, excluding no one. For the aggressive worker, however, the preparation is long and demanding, as we said. Unlike the passive person, the aggressive worker engages in provocation by challenging the negative. There is a major and very serious difference between defending one's own security and the hazard of initiating aggression to demolish and to debase an opponent."

Adversarial Awareness

"Now, let's concentrate on the interests of the passive person and omit what the aggressive worker does. The fact is, of course, that we do not overlook his presence as one among us. We are only setting aside discussion about the steps of his preparation to engage in aggressive confrontation. Otherwise, he too is a passive person, the same as everyone else.

"What I will say next may seem as a contradiction. Yet, it is not. One laboring in one's own defense, to some degree, is performing the work of the aggressive worker. In different words, an aphorism leveled by a passive person to dispel a negative presence may be similar to an aphorism by the aggressive person for the same purpose. The difference, nevertheless, is profound in that the passive person is doing this for a defensive reason; whereas the aggressive worker is doing it on a head-on clash against an opponent whom the worker has incited, provoked, and challenged. The difference here is one of *intent*.

"Remember again that everyone is entitled to defend oneself. But, to go out of the way in order to pursue and to confront requires far more serious and intensive preparation, if not outright the special calling to do so. This explanation highlights one of the issues of awareness. Everyone must know and understand the circumstances under which certain actions take place. The internal attitude and sentiment of a person who postures in either of the two ways— passive or aggressive—are quite different. The engagement is quite different, although the ultimate goal is the same. Purpose, intent, awareness, integrity of thought, and depth of faith: all are critical ingredients in dealing with a negative force. That type of opponent is also very well prepared. A person who engages in the activity must know that the challenge is reciprocal—a two-way street—as the response comes back in a most insidious and cunning way.

"Awareness falls under two categories that function together and interact with each other. There must be awareness of what is happening to oneself—that is, receiving; and there must be awareness of what one is doing to respond to what is happening—that is, projecting. Liken it if you will to a radio talk-show dealing with an adversarial subject; except that in this case, it is not just talk that is involved. Two parties exchange remarks, and each defends a position while disparaging that of the other. The process requires the participants to receive and to deliver. Each must be aware of what is coming or what is heard, in order to be able with equal awareness to form a successful response. Each must be aware of the effect of an incoming remark, considering one's own opinions, convictions, attitudes, sentiments, principles, and the like. The reaction to that evaluation will determine the kind of response and its impact on the opponent. Unless one is able to remain aware of all the nuances in the exchange, the result will be victory for the opponent. An added somber concern regarding the confrontation is not only the critical awareness of what is being *said* but more so of what, at the same time, is being *done*. "Nothing I've said is new. Exchanges are always at play in human relations, whether it is a radio-talk program or a simple conversation among friends. What I am trying to point out is the importance of attentiveness to the significant issue of awareness. The difference, however, between a simple conversational event, a radio-talk show, or a political debate etc. and an exchange with a negative force is an extraordinary one. The latter is not an interaction between kindred principals such as speaker to speaker, man to man, and human to human. The elements of the exchange here are very different, and the outcome of the involvement is set to be final. The objective is the capitulation of the most precious gift in human life: *the soul.*

"It should be clear that the question of awareness is very important when involved in spiritual matters. Nothing can be left to chance, and nothing can go unattended. As I said earlier, there is no room for inaptitude, ignorance, arrogance, or failing in faith".

"I can see where alertness has to be very high" the older son muttered in a detached and casual way. In reality, he was at the moment reflecting on the seriousness of the conditions the father had described. His words were just an unconscious echo of another apparent soliloquy going on in his mind.

"To be sure" added the sister. "It would appear that with all the hazards lurking around, one would want to be dressed in armor."

"Absolutely" said the father. "And do you know? You have said the right thing; because that's what we should be talking about next."

The older brother had just come out from the privacy of his thoughts. He had a question. "Before we go on" he said "isn't it unrealistic to think that every moment of our life humanity is in a state of battle? I can't agree that this is true."

"Of course, not...yet, as I told you earlier the working of the intruder is subtle and devious. For some persons of certain sensitivity, the attack may be severe and penetrating, whereas, for others, evidently the greatest part of humanity, the attacks are manifested as problems of decision-making in social behavior, ethics, and morals. Temptations are a constant in every person's life. Of that, there is no doubt. Can you see then, how in such instances the intruder is ever-present?"

"Yes, I take your point. Even the strong persons can be undermined in some way or another" the youngster responded.

"Very much so...and we have so many examples of reputable and respected people going astray" the father confirmed.

"All right,...let us continue then with sister's observation about being dressed in armor."

Personal Awareness

"Dressed in armor is a great way of putting it! The subject of awareness mentioned so far had to do more with what was being said than what was being done. Remember,...the mind games we talked about? However, concealed behind the words there is a more sinister intent. It is something of which we should be very much aware...And I just touched on this only a moment ago; but, let's focus a little more.

"Words can influence people because they affect emotions, sentiments, and deep-rooted convictions. These influences translate into physical reactions that can be either beneficial or detrimental. So, not only one must be aware of incoming remarks, which is needed in order to formulate effective responses; it is also very important to police such remarks in order to know what effect they are causing on us in terms of our well-being mentally, psychologically, and physically. And, when dealing with the negative force, you will remember I said it comes back on the two-way street with insidiousness and cunning. The object of that ill-intended return is to destroy the integrity of the person and debase, vanquish, and ravish one's soul by any means possible—whether through doubt in one's faith, through sophistry, or even through depletion by sapping or taxing physical energy and the will; and surprisingly, not lacking in smooth-talking, humor, and hypocrisy besides outright aggression. The whole panoply is there.

"We have; therefore, two categories of awareness as relates to incoming or receiving and outgoing or projecting or broadcasting of remarks.

"And, under these two categories we identify two classifications: One is the intellectual exchanges of what is said—mind games. That is, 'Who is smarter?'

"The other is the action or what is intended to be done to us physically and mentally and psychologically.

"With all this at hand, we can proceed with a better understanding of why the expression *one would want to be dressed in armor* is very fitting. Although, we would not be content to lose our prowess in the intelligence ploy—mind games—the more devastating loss is the one that demolishes our mental, psychological, or physical integrity. We can think, of course, of armor protecting our intellectual competence; but more appropriate is an armor that protects us physically and psychologically.

"It is not excluded to suffer physical discomforts, ailments, and diseases as well as psychological disturbances when attacked by insidious negative intrusion. After all, the chief purpose of such intrusion is disruption of normalcy and the introduction of mayhem. The final play-out against one and one's surroundings are unknown. Yet, two things will result: One is, as stated earlier, that a confrontation resolution will always take place. And the second is that in the very last analysis the ultimate loser is the intruder ... and knows it. The true yearning of the intruder is the return to the Light. However, stubbornness and misplaced pride supersedes better judgment, and the devastation continues. The enlistment of innocent souls by deceit or capture is a way of self-justification that, after all, the negative existence is valid: with so many souls being on that side. It is a pathetic defense stance.

"When next we discuss defensive awareness, this point of proper defense will come up again.

"Evidence of what occurs when negative interference manifests itself does not bode well. The tendency is to consider intrusion on isolated or personal levels such as demonic possessions and the like. Yet, it should not be discounted that negative intrusion impacts conditions at a very large scale. Such can be, for example, wars, genocides, economic disasters, terrorism, political corruption, and other such events that begin through the actions of one or a few individuals. The intrusion, in other words, may have a start on a personal level in order to be initiated, but is designed to expand and affect even the whole world. Persons in positions of leadership are as vulnerable as other individuals and can be manipulated to trigger massive disturbances and havoc. The more evident goal of these intrusions is the ultimate capitulation of the human soul whether in small or very large numbers.

"Therefore, the ultimate goal of all protection must always be the salvation of every human soul.

"Toward this end, let us look further into the notion of awareness and identify its essence. A public warning in general recommending preparation against a physical disaster such as an earthquake, for example, without listing the requisite protection specifics is meaningless. The same is true in the spiritual arena when advising one to be aware.

"Awareness relates to the general understanding that dangers may be present; but also implies that particular steps need to be taken in response to the alert.

"Earlier in our discussion I stated that this gathering was not intended to teach the particulars for preparation and performance of an aggressive worker. I will, however, touch on awareness in relation to the passive mode. Let us call this *personal awareness,* as it is something that affects the personal welfare of the individual.

"The matter of personal awareness is described in one of three ways: The person is unaware of what is happening; the person is aware something is happening but denies the fact; the person is aware something is happening and accepts it.

"The latter of the three is the worst situation, insofar as the afflicted person has a choice to reject but instead invites. Refusal may be linked to weak mental aptitude; lack of maturity; personal ignorance or ignorance within the surrounding social environment; or willingness due to the preference for malice, which is effectively an acceptance. Other possible reasons may also exist.

"The complexity of a willing acceptance is not because of the willingness of the afflicted person. It is instead the influence of the vexing negative force that makes the person believe to be willing. This condition, by definition, places the person in the first of the three cases listed above. That is, the person is unaware that he is misinterpreting that of which he is aware and willing to accept.

"It is difficult to deal with a person unaware of the prevailing circumstances, because while there is clarity in their mental aptitude, it is not easy to convey to and to convince such person that there is a problem.

"The person who is willing to accept assistance—one who rejects the unwanted presence—is, of course, the least complex to receive help.

"Having said all this, it may appear that the above approaches relate more to psychological treatments than to the spiritual realm of removal of negative influences. This perception is because of reference to some conscious recognition by the afflicted person regarding their condition; and, because of reference to the positive or negative input contributed by the afflicted person's mind. However, it is not so. The spiritual problem and the interference by a negative force are independent conditions within the person. To be sure, such readings are often confusing and misleading; but they also become discernable in due time. It must be remembered that neither implemented psychology principles nor spiritual practice are sciences: they are both an art; albeit the former uses empirical observations and depends on the very source it attempts to explain.

Defensive Awareness

"The art so referenced in this discussion is neither the exclusive domain of psychology nor of the inclination to spirituality. It is a universal gift to everyone and thus also to every afflicted person who suffers the impudence and danger of a negative intrusion. The focus of this art, however, should not be on the outcome of intrusion—or sensationalism as mentioned—but on its prevention. It is regrettable that so much false attention, theatrics, pretense, even derision and abuse have been leveled against the most sacred part of human existence: the human soul.

"That which is needed is the bolstering and not the weakening of man's faith.

"Abhorrent literature, films, pseudo-clergy, sordid television monstrosities; all do little to edify the human soul and much to break down a sustaining and deep faith that preserves life in healthy, vibrant, and refined form.

"The best defense for man is to initiate a vision of self-immersion into a luminous purity of sublime *white light,* formed about in a surrounding sphere extending at least an arm's length in every direction, including above and below one's physical person. Broad awareness is a requisite to convince the mind that one is not alone within this empowering sacred vicinity. Any perception of an unwanted influence must be repelled and must be ordered to depart. Beyond this, however, such negative presence must be forcefully mandated to seek the universal source of Light to receive knowledge and education; and must never return again. These words suffice. Objectionable language is not to be used, for it degrades the user to the level of the intruder and the circumstances are reversed. Rejection must be final. No negative force exists that exceeds the power of The Creator. The command to access the Light has an irresistible and compelling effect.

Its power supersedes any of the designs by the negative force. Such a force knows that it never has and never will subdue the Creative Light from whence all life proceeds. It is neither the voice nor the command of the person that triggers obedience. Self-conviction is the cause, and the command reflects and articulates that for which the negative force thirsts. Not only the intended victim is helped, but also the negative intruder is liberated. Failure to assert the command negates any effect on the intruder, which in all probability will remain near and about—more active and in greater defiance. Practice of this releasing procedure is fundamental. It is also wise to apply it in disagreeable situations when an adverse presence is sensed, yet not perceived in full. Also, one must not be complaisant when in a favorable or peaceful state; for it is in such relaxed and unsuspecting moments that intrusion may also occur. The constancy of the method is never exhaustible.

"It is significant to emphasize the lonesomeness hazard in connection with intrusion vulnerability. The subject can be approached from the viewpoint of individualism. However, this does not imply support for an individualistic or self-centered, egotistical personality. The term refers to one's ability of self-awareness as a separate individual among other persons. And individualism must not be confused with *aloneness*. Also, to be lonely does not make one an individual. And to be in a great crowd does not deprive one of being an individual.

"The important point made here is that a person isolated from the company of others does not lose the sense of self-identity. This is basic in every human being. The emotional input that occurs, however, may distort this fundamental cognizance and cause the person to feel separated and even deserted. A contributor to that input is one's mental perception; whereby the person's imagination begins to nourish feelings of detachment. This in turn promotes the notion of lonesomeness, which compounds into a state of loneliness. The latter is the most vulnerable condition that negative intrusion prefers. The person suffers a dual weakness: One is the sensation of abandonment by others, and the other is the desire for companionship—any companionship. This spells danger: which is the open door for the unqualified acceptance of any visitor or ultimate settler.

"It is thus important to encourage the sense of individualism and the habit of self-acceptance, confidence, and identity as a means of occupying all vacant space within oneself. Physical isolation should not be interpreted as a sign of lonesomeness. The understanding of a consciousness negates the feeling of emptiness and forestalls on the ability of intrusion into a space already occupied.

"Now, here is the basic approach that in practical terms precedes visualizing and experiencing the encompassing white light. In order to institute and to sustain the presence of the enveloping light, it must first be internalized. Begin with a vision of a concentrated brilliant white light in the mind's eye. See the light there first. It forms the foundation or the root for the expansion of the larger external surrounding light. Although the external light may seem to dissipate—but not lost—during normal human activity and attention to other matters; the internal focused and intense light remains intact and is experienced without interruption. It is logical that one's mental process attaches instantly to one's self-awareness. An external environment includes many other random variables that must be processed through the sensual complex and the emotional system of the person. Thus, the surrounding light may appear to dissipate—but not lost—depending on the intensity of focus as affected by external interferences.

"The white light in the mind's eye attains constant presence with persistent practice. It can be born in the mind with equal permanence as the ring on the finger. Once this presence is established, the person can engage in other activities, including, for example, thought challenging conversations. Contrary to what may appear to be the case, the presence of the light is not a distraction but a source of inspiration, confidence, and judgment, as it tends to negate wrong-doing. It is, as stated, the staging point from where the enveloping light begins. The latter does not originate in the external environment; and, although it may be imagined to exist, unless born of the soul and embodied in the mind it is not authentic. The source of the expanded light is grounded in the soul. The realization of this experience is irreversible and a gift for life: it generates hope, a positive approach to life, the mitigation of anxiety; the broadening of the mind; and among other similar attributes it promotes a state of heartiness that is reflected in one's physical radiance. To appear younger: it is sad to lift the face and not the spirit; for it is spirit first.

"It must also always be remembered that once a person is cleansed, an even more attractive target becomes available for attack. Thus, it is necessary to remain ever more vigilant against future intrusion; and the application of the protective process described above should be continuous. We have already established that the negative aspect of our created life exists from the beginning in tandem with our positive and desirable nature. Therefore, we must not view as a chore the way our existence is arranged. We should accept it as a fact of life the same as we do our breathing. In such a setting, the practice of self-protection must be accepted as a constant."

The last remarks caused the sister to raise the question: "Since the arrangement seems to be so fixed, are we to think that all happenings in life are preset? Yet, in *The Great Age*, I remember that fatalism was downgraded. So, it must be that the will of the person has a lot to do with what happens."

"Yes, it does" the father responded, "and it was pretty clear that the writing supported that position."

"Hold on a second." The older boy again lifted forward his palm in a gesture to halt the conversation and to emphasize his point. He went on: "We've got that negative influence to think about. You said it's always out there, lurking and looking to invest itself into the world and to cause havoc. With the way things are so firmly set, are we to believe that more bad occurs than good? Or is it the other way around? And, I too say: Is it all preset and there is nothing we can do about it?"

The youngest now jumped into the fray, "Is all that happens, good or bad, linked to the will for good, or to evil?"

This last question offered the father the chance he wanted in order to cover all the questions:

"OK, we'll take up the last question. And let's see if we can satisfy all our concerns.

"I will say that in principle what prevails is a mix. We all know that good and bad are always active. The negative is bent on causing harm and destruction; while the positive favors tranquility; providing it remains vigilant and competent to defend. A hypothetical example, I will describe, will likely will symbolize with some accuracy the realities of our current life experience.

"First, let's visualize in our mind a river running downhill, where at a certain spot it becomes a waterfall as it funnels through a narrow rock formation prior to dropping. The riverbed in the upper terrain begins to widen because of the narrows. Over time, a large lake is formed as tree trunks from the wooded area with debris from the surrounding vegetation drift to the narrow channel and block it. There is also a colony of some very productive beavers at work, and a natural dam is formed. However, the dam does not hold indefinitely. The volume of water reaches critical mass and pushes the debris down the precipice. The sudden break releases a large amount of water that floods the immediate area at the foot of the falls. The inability of the ground to absorb the water quickly aggravates the flooding.

"There are many boats in the upper lake with people fishing and sailing, and many people below the falls camping and fishing. The situation is a disaster. Several persons below drown, and others are hurt. Much property is damaged. The lake-crowd is also seriously affected when some of the boats are drawn into the current and either crash against the rocks or are sucked down the falls.

"Now, let's modify the scenario. We'll say that the natural dam formed by the debris and the beavers was a very good one and capable to last for a great many years. Mother Nature had done an excellent job. Nevertheless, this excellent structure did break one day. The cause, however, was not the pressure from the excessive volume of water. The cause was the malicious and thoughtless act of some unscrupulous persons who took it upon themselves to destroy the dam and widen the lake bottom in order to expand their land holdings.

"This fictional account is not meant to involve us in a discussion of morality. Our attention should go to the sustained beauty and peace that had prevailed and to the destruction that was wrought upon it.

"Everything was normal. People and nature had followed their usual course. Yet, everything was taken for granted. Vigilance had not been considered necessary until adversity struck. And adversity proved to come from the very midst of the community. Had there been provision to guard against a negative contingency, disaster would have been averted.

"Let us liken this example to life as we know it. The natural way of our being is replete with moments of tranquility, safety, and continuity. After all, humanity has been around for thousands of years. We have much for which to be thankful. Except for the deprived areas of the world—an error of our own making—many persons live in considerable comfort and security. Nature provides constancy of climate; ground firmness on which to live; even the opportunity for water-bound, air-bound, and recently possible space-bound existence. Natural disasters, as severe as they often are, still allow space for us to continue.

"We also have in our midst the occasional if not frequent devised interference from the negative force. Again, this intrusion and the life described above are not the outcome of fatalism but the way we have been structured. It is a condition that we must accept with maturity and courage. To be sure, there will be malefactors bent on breaking dams and doing harm to others for their own questionable reasons. Our attitude, however, must be one of cognizance, discretion, and constant vigilance in dealing with such realities.

"In *The Great Age* was mentioned the willingness to assert the will in order to confront and to deal with reality. It is the acceptance of life as given. Adversity in physical life is not to be laid at the feet of the Creator, as though the Creator somehow betrays the created. Faith in the Creator relates to the higher consciousness. Life at the physical level is cast as it is: the same as the river described in its normal flow and natural dam-building. Negative intrusions are acts of the unwanted who are the destroyers of the dam, whom man must learn to police. Constructive contributions are the labor of the edifiers, as portrayed in the enterprising beavers and keepers of the dam…"

An expression of contentment was in the face of the youngsters. The anecdote appears to have done the job. Everything became focused: the physical and spiritual worlds; creation; good against bad; faith and the lack of it; willingness and the will; and all those other notions that were discussed. It all made sense, including the idea of the Spheres—an issue that demanded great originality and creative imagination.

A Peek into the Fourth Sphere

"It's clear that we have devoted much time dealing with the subject on an abstract basis." The father continued. "I am inclined to believe that all of you would be quite pleased to have an opportunity

112

of a sneak preview into the fourth Sphere, as it were. Well, I cannot achieve an actual entry even for my own benefit; and at best, what I can do is embolden my imagination to a degree that I can feel as though I have accessed that level of consciousness or awareness.

"Here then is an approach that we can use; and with which I'm hopeful you too will experience a degree of achievement. Are you ready and willing to journey?"

All three nodded to the affirmative with an evident look of excitement and inquisitiveness.

"OK...let's try it! Let's all gather around the computer screen."

They all shuffled their chairs around their father who sat in front of the monitor. He started the system and began a specific search. All three youngsters leaned in close for a better view of the screen. He was ready by the time they settled down and then continued:

"You can see I've brought up a beautiful panoramic view of the blue sky. The idea is for you to disregard the hilly outline in the horizon and the few scattered clouds that are showing. Try to focus on the clear blue sky as much as you can. Take your time doing this, until you have identified with the sky and feel that you are part of it. Consider if you will that you are in an aircraft or spacecraft flying high and free. You are traveling at the speed of your preference. Make every attempt to detach yourself from your present environment in this room or from your seat. Just simply fly around in the vastness of that gorgeous sky. Continue this for a few moments until you feel the sensation of flight and lightness, and that the sky that you are seeing is the real sky.

"Just enjoy it!...Let your imagination take hold.

"Now, very suddenly, break away from that image and the experience! Immediately, think of the real sky, the natural sky outside. Keep looking at the monitor and right away tell yourself that the sky in the screen is just what it is—only a lit-up picture. Also, at the same time think of the real sky above you.

"That sudden awakening more likely will bring to focus in your mind how little, how fictitious and tangible the screen sky actually is. Yet, the sky outside is real, it's large, and it's a living sky!

"This simple exercise produces an example of how we can think of the natural sky in comparison to the true sky of the higher Sphere.

"Try going a step further and experience the fourth consciousness, or the reality of the Sphere that envelops our physical level.

"This time, use the same procedure. However, your imagination will need to be much more aggressive. The success of this trial depends on your ability to project and to visualize.

"Go outside on a clear day with a blue sky. Immerse yourself in free and relaxing travel in it. Do this for a few moments. Then, just as you did before, suddenly break away from that experience and acknowledge this sky as very physical, while at the same time you visualize above it another larger blue sky surrounding this one. Feel at that moment how physical and how material this sky is in comparison to that higher, pure, and spiritual sky that is there."

The silence of the youngsters was clear evidence of how wrapped up they had become in what they heard. Their agile minds were able to absorb the impact of the allegations; and without a doubt they were already planning their next venture in the experiment.

The power of their imagination had taken firm hold ...

"It's time for us now to close this meeting until the next one" the father continued. "I want to leave you with one more thought, however, which is the message that underlies all we've talked about. Think of it this way: It is difficult enough for us to imagine let alone to acknowledge that the fourth Sphere is there waiting for us. Nevertheless, despite the fact that we've come short of achieving such progress, we should live our lives with great humility and faith in our Creator, and with much joyful enthusiasm and anticipation of a higher life.

"Just think of this as well: If it is so invigorating and exciting for us to recognize and to enter the fourth Sphere; imagine how much more eventful it will be, considering three additional Spheres after the fourth one, and six more after those. Humanity has a long, very long way to go to reach the zenith or the state of pure awareness. A condition such as that does not portend a meaningless time ahead. There is also no need to be impatient about it, if we think of how much more there is for us to experience and to enjoy on our way to our destination. We have good reason, therefore, always to feel young, hopeful, and alive."

These closing thoughts marked the end of this gathering. All through the course of these meetings there was never an occasion when the youngsters were deprived of their interests and activities. These were fostered with much diligence. The object was to instill in them discretion, balance in their thought process, and strength in their character.

PART IV

Last Encounter

Questioning the Premise

Time seems to have gone by quickly. Several weeks had passed since the last meeting. The children had been absorbed in their schoolwork and other social activities, while both parents carried on with their own responsibilities. For the father, however, there was a stayed concern in back of his mind to see the task finished. He knew that all was not yet complete with the children. On the other hand, he also felt the need not to impose himself on them and press further on the subjects they had discussed. Time was important for all those issues to be assimilated in the young active minds. Any insistence or repetition would have been counterproductive, as it would have caused boredom if not outright dislike and ultimate rejection. He was patient.

So, school times and the other usual family events went on as in any other home. Birthdays, anniversaries, and holidays, all received their due observance. Prayers were a staple activity.

The summer break that followed was as active this time as were several others before. This involved considerable travel for pleasure and enjoyment and for educational purposes. The relaxed atmosphere and unique experiences involving varied environments and panoramic views, changing time zones, climate, and people. All were instrumental in producing a broader, more creative and more inquisitive mind frame and attitude for everyone in the family. To be sure, the stage was being set for the next encounter. Yet this time, not because of the father's suggestion, but due to the children's own initiative. Without a doubt, all those prior meetings had affected the youngsters' thinking and how they reflected on life. In other words, they had developed a certain philosophical competence that gave them an edge in adjusting and dealing objectively with changing circumstances.

This was the setting that appeared most promising to the father. He remained alert for the proper moment to arrive. And as he had anticipated, the moment did come when, by their own comments, the children began to broach the subject of life in relation to the planets, the stars, and the universe.

It is most inspiring for the average person to find oneself high up in the mountains, such as for example in the Rockies or the Western Sierras, on a clear night gazing at the richness of the universe. The experience renders it impossible not to contemplate, and given the circumstances, not to discuss the wonder of creation and to acknowledge the presence of the Supreme Creator. This is so, even if one attempts to conceal in arrogance, one's comparative inadequacy by declaring atheism or a scientific knowledge of all creation.

The older brother who as we know was quite well-versed in the arrangement and location of the stars and the planets—albeit self-taught—at that point, began to remark about their various positions, characteristics, and movements. He spoke about them with great familiarity and confidence, revealing a considerable amount of knowledge. He took everyone by surprise with his ability to respond to almost every question thrown at him. And indeed, the questions kept coming with enthusiasm and impatience, as they all believed in the urgency of their own particular focus at the moment. Such human frailty in behavior, of course, was not at all uncommon, considering the emotional effect caused by the grandeur and vastness of that heavenly panorama. He went on to speak about the Milky Way and the galaxies; and he even pointed out in the darkness of the night the earth's own shadow cast out into space by the effect of the sun being behind the earth. That particular experience was very engaging, for it empowers the individual with a strong feeling of personal involvement in the working of the universe. One's perception changes: It is no longer a matter of how some distant extraterrestrial influence affects the earth, but how a visible and real influence from one's own earth, underneath one's own feet, can cast its influence upon the vastness of space.

It was the children's time, and they were aware of it. There was no rush to meet the next day's obligations. Early retirement was not the issue, and the general mood was to remain awake and to talk.

This is the opportunity, the father thought. *But still, I'm not going to chance it. Let them approach me. This way, they will not feel pressured or compromised. I'll wait.*

His estimate was correct. The experience of the evening was more of a bursting out than a mild cause of the dialogue that followed. The heavens and the stars triggered it. Over the past several months, the children had gotten into conversations on their own about all that had been discussed in the early meetings. Although such discussions were sporadic, they nevertheless did occur. Small wonder then, that when the conversation started up, the remarks and the questions came on hard and heavy.

The salvo was a joint venture between the daughter and the youngest. The boy spoke first. His curt words and tone would have caused a Spartan to cringe: "OK, I see the stars and I see the big universe. So, where do I go outside of it?"

And the daughter, speaking over her brother's voice, remarked: "If this beautiful universe is just the residual, as you told us: how is it that we are so insignificant in comparison? It seems to me that we have so little power over so many things that are happening."

The barrage caused pause to the father. He had not anticipated as penetrating a kickoff as this. Yet, it became clear to him at once that he was dealing with prepared minds that were anxious to challenge and to be challenged. At the same time, he felt comfortable that from this point forward he was free to speak to the children in adult terms. That is, spoon-feeding the fundamentals was over.

He began with a response that would address both inquiries, while opening the way to expand on the notion of the seven Spheres: "I believe that you will each be satisfied with the same response, since your questions are in essence related. Whether or not the universe is immense does not affect its nature. The transition from it is an escape from its size and composition: an escape that annuls all time and distance. Matter and man are of the same nature. You will remember that both come from one source; although the human and the animal components are enriched with spirit, while the material is lacking. The latter is the residual. So, the escape from this dual world—which in reality is one—means that the separation is total. Jesus made precise reference to this when in Matthew 10:39 he admonishes: *He that findeth his life shall lose it: and he that loseth his life for my sake shall find it.* Dimensions, time, reaction of the senses are all values of the natural dominion. Such a dominion has an unforgiving binding power that relents only when exhausted by its own wear, such as when life ends through normal course—voluntary termination having other implications."

"You make it all sound so small and so uncomplicated; but I look up there and everything looks so far away and so huge," remarked again his younger son.

And the older of the brothers now jumped in, adding, "That's a fact. Even science finds it difficult to give answers to so many things that are out there."

"Yes, you are both correct. Comparatively, it's much, much less that science knows about what really exists. This, however, is the challenge of this life that cannot be denied; and, should not be denied. Yet, this does not negate the existence of an even more complex condition that surrounds us. Our obligation while we are in this stage of life is to meet our commitment in the fullest measure and with the proper attitude and enthusiasm. There is much to enjoy while doing so. Time and space, as large as they are, should not be a deterrent to discouraging us.

"Let's take, for example, our very presence up here in these tall mountains. We spoke about those forbidding peaks we saw all around us earlier today. They looked so far away and so inaccessible from the highway, as though no human had ever approached them

122

before. This may be true for most of them. However, some have been visited with much frequency, and there are access roads that lead right up to them. Tomorrow we will be doing exactly that. We will be driving there. And when we arrive, you will be surprised how familiar and ordinary those ominous peaks will become. You will be able to see them up close and even to touch them. And they will be for you nothing but simple rocks as any other rocks. Even the pebbles on the ground around you will speak of their simple existence, laying there for years on end. That which was formidable will be reduced to an ordinary sight."

"I have a suspicion as to why you are telling us this" interrupted the young miss. "Just the same though, we would love to hear it. You're probably leading up to something else."

"Wait,... it seems you're getting ahead of me; but I don't mind. You're right though; and I believe you will agree with me on this. When I speak of the strange becoming familiar it is because it's important to scale down the mystery of the material universe. As I said, there is no doubt that much too much exists in the world that we know little or nothing about. That ignorance, however, should not be the cause for excessive awe, denial, or inertia. Nor should it be a source for presumptiveness or arrogance. The attitude should be one of moderation with a great deal of initiative, humility, and constructive anticipation.

"Let me put it this way ..." however, before he could finish his sentence the youngest interrupted:

"But wait, wait a moment...We are now getting away from the question I have. You mentioned before what Jesus said about finding life by losing it. What has that to do with strange things that become familiar things? We are jumping from one subject to another."

The observation he made was correct in all appearances. Yet, in real terms, the father knew that what had just happened was that the whole project—meetings, talks, dialogues, etc.—all had now reached the limit. The question his young son had raised brought to view the very foundation upon which his whole effort was built. He paused for a few moments to gather his thoughts and to set the strategy he would use to bring forth his points.

The Larger View

"All right, you make a very good point" the father admitted. "Let's go back and revisit the Master's admonishment. Nothing he ever said was without purpose or meaning—a deep meaning, to be sure. Before I expand on this, however, I hope that you will try to see how all the individual subjects we discuss are linked together. In the long run you will discern how the notion of the strange becoming familiar is very much related to the notion of someone finding life by losing life. Just try to keep in mind the overall cohesiveness of multiple parts. Stop me if I lose you along the way. It is important not to break the sequence of thoughts, because we will build one thought upon another and there cannot be any break in the continuity. Also, when using the word strange, it does not refer to something peculiar; it refers to something that is unfamiliar.

"Let us begin with present life as the keystone of human awareness". It's simple enough to do. In other words, we are as we know ourselves to be: living in this life, in this environment, conscious of what we are, of what we do, feel, and think. Now, let us say we are convinced we must raise our general condition to a higher level and that we work up to it. This may include refining our behavior, culture, education, physical condition, material status, as well as pursuing a major spiritual transformation. In effect, we attempt to elevate our status to a new standard, at least in our own mind, which means that for our own sake—and I stress, for our own sake—we search to find a new life and to dismiss or lose the old one. In actual terms, however, even if the objective is reached, no shift has occurred beyond the present life other than a commendable personal refinement. This presumed gain includes any perceived spiritual advancement one achieves under one's own initiative and for one's own sake. The net effect is that no life of grace has been appended other than personal physical, material, or moral gain.

"There is another aspect to be considered in the admonishment. This time, we shall assume one's literal loss of life. In such a case there may be more than just physical loss. This is to say that, in an incidence of loss of life, if faith in a superior force is absent; there is risk of loss involved for the very soul as well.

"The second stipulation that Jesus includes in his admonishment provides the manner how to deal with the above shortcoming. He points out that action should be taken for his sake, which fact secures for us the ultimate advantage of finding life.

There was silence for a few moments, as the children reflected on the last statements. The sister then broke the lull by saying, "But, this may be true for those who believe in Jesus. What about people that are not his followers?"

"Well, the message that he brought was not linking faith to anything physical. The thrust of his message is universal for any and all human beings, regardless of social affiliations and attachments to institutions, organizations, groups, and all such. The essence of universality is inherent in the ascending spheres we discussed in our earlier meetings. For those who do follow him, the object of his incarnation was to make an abstract message comprehensible in human terms. His identity was from the outset not intended to be in his physical makeup, but in the spirit and power of his conveyance.

This is why he submitted to sacrifice in order to confirm and exemplify the principle of finding life through faith.

The older son now inquired, "Yes, I can see how important this is. And, somehow, I also see how this can tie in with things that are familiar and others that are not. But can we hear more about it?"

"Yes" came the combined approval of the other siblings.

"All right,...let me see first if I can present the basic notion in a straightforward understandable way. Once we have that in place, we may want to become a bit more sophisticated about the whole principle. Eventually, we would want to touch on the seven Spheres once more: but this time with an enhanced understanding.

"This practice is an excellent way to keep both mind and soul in harmony; to keep a vibrant mental attitude; to feel younger; and also, to project such an appearance. The actual aging process is not reversible. Yet, the ability to muster up renewed drive is achievable by everyone. You have all seen the artistic representation of the Seven Spheres. Beyond the art, however, lies the inspirational quality of the design that assists even the most advanced person in achieving higher awareness every time it is used. It is a handsome item that promises a lifetime of inspiration and usage. We will come to that later. At this time our attention must be turned to our immediate objective.

"You have heard of the expression that *familiarity breeds contempt*. This is often quite true. Contempt, however, should best be substituted with consideration and respect. Even in the most adverse cases of formality, better results accrue by due consideration than by contempt. A realistic view reveals that in each case contempt for what has become familiar outweighs and outlives the original urge for its discovery. This is because once discovery is consummated no need exists for further discovery. The result of discovery, however, is precious and should not be relegated to contempt. The principle applies in social relations as well as in scientific discovery. Our world is built on constructive progression; but it can also be destroyed by its corresponding regression, if we are contemptuous of that which has been discovered.

"We should not be surprised that our universe, as vast and mysterious as it appears, is in the final analysis part of our natural existence. The mysterious mountain peaks we spoke about are the mysterious peaks of space in the form of planets, stars, and galaxies. Objects, which when unveiled as to their nature, will also be familiar things that have always been and will continue to be a part of us.

This brings us to the issue of finding life. The question, however, is, what life? Is it the same life within which the search occurred; or is it another kind of which we know nothing? How can life at another planet, in this or in any other galaxy, be outside the constraints of this physical world? If such a life is discovered in another galaxy, all that will have occurred is a physical variation of the same life and a loss of the prior arrangement—this, despite the dramatic and extraordinary character of the event. Once such discovery and resettlement are realized, the familiarity of that physical environment, albeit unique perhaps, will be treated with the corresponding usual contempt.

"The life committed to humanity by Jesus, which life is sought by man for the Master's sake, is also unfamiliar. Potential familiarity with it, however, should not now encourage or deny our prospect of contempt. The reason is that we know nothing about that life since it is not within the confines of our present domain. Consider the possibility, for example, that contempt in that setting may not even exist, let alone to be practiced."

The usual pause of silence followed the father's remarks. Then, in a slow manner as though dragging out his words, while gazing thoughtfully into space, the youngest challenged the father with this comment: "It seems that first you separate things for being different, and then turn around and make them one again. What are you saying exactly?"

"Um,…I believe I know what you're asking; but what about the rest of you?" The father wanted to know where the other two siblings stood. He was concerned all four were on the same track. The stuff coming up was even more demanding. "Do you grasp what he's asking, and do you agree?" In a simultaneous nod they both signaled agreements.

"All right then, we should continue."

CHAPTER II

A New Approach

Changing the Perspective

The father began his explanation with this: "The world as we know it is the only reference we have. Our only recourse we have when attempting to describe the unknown is to depend on the known or at least on what we think is known.

"So, it is impossible to embark on a discourse in such matters and not rely on terms that define what is known. It is fortunate at least that we have devised words such as *unknown, unfamiliar, strange, uncharted,* etc. Words are not the origin of thoughts. It is the other way around: Thoughts are the foundation of words. Without a preexisting thought, there exists no basis to create a corresponding symbol, a word that represents it. Such symbols are the words we have established; and the richer our thought arsenal, the richer our language becomes.

"Words then, reveal to us that of which we are aware, or that of which we have a thought, including the perception of the unknown. The school of *nominalism* considers words of general meaning to be just that: symbolic expressions or descriptions of occurring thoughts that have no basis in *reality*. However, the problem with that line of thinking is that the so-called reality is its current Sphere. The doctrine is in a position of self-definition—which is a blind position, considering the far greater vision of life in the seven Spheres. On the other hand, the school of *realism* also suffers disadvantage in asserting the reality of objects independent of whether they are perceived or not. However, it is not known how this can be confirmed outside the process of thinking, which thinking is limited within its own confines. Furthermore, is it not reasonable to consider that other forms of life may also be impelled by the unknown? The characteristic of both curiosity and fear prompted by some unknown is observed in many creatures. Yet, in our very own environment we lack the knowledge of the nature of the influence upon such creatures.

"I bring all this up in order to underscore the reasoning ability that favors human nature. Nevertheless, this ability has its limitations that confine the extent to which man can exceed himself or his environment. Coupled together, the ability to reason about the unknown and the sense of confinement, they produce the urge for humans to search and to discover. This cognizance of simultaneous ability and inability is the driving force that propels humans into constant desire for challenge. Yet, all this energy is structured to remain within the same framework. One can say that there are two categories of the unknown: a) the physical unknown, including outer space, the stars, the galaxies, etc. and b) the total unknown, or the ideal, the spiritual. The former is almost definable, for it can be extrapolated on the basis of known physical attributes. The latter is a ... blank, which when attempted to be described only becomes adulterated with elements of the known. After all, those are the only tools we have with which to describe anything!

"Therefore, this is the reason you found me separating and joining the values discussed. In other words, I am compelled to admit that I have limitations under which I am able to convey my thoughts to you. Beyond that point, it all depends on your own ability and mental acuity to grasp the meaning of the unknown to which I may refer. Factual evidence, theoretical science, and all disciplines can be taught. Spiritual growth is a gift of grace.

"And here is the crux of this whole rather involved conversation: For the Master's sake: When one finds life by losing life, it is not treated with contempt; for it is an outcome not confined within the familiar."

"It seems to me that we have come to the point that I anticipated earlier ..." concluded the older son. "Our whole discussion going back several weeks centered on the meaning of the Spheres, which I think has much to do with everything you just discussed. Is it possible now to return to that subject?"

"Yes, it is. And I too believe that the moment is right." The father agreed. "Consider, however, that we were never separated from the central notion of the Spheres."

"Then," the sister remarked "can you expand more on the subject of how we relate to them?"

"OK, I'll do that. But first, to whom are you referring when you say, 'how we relate to them'—are you speaking about us here at our meeting; or are you referring to mankind as a whole when you say, 'we'?"

"No, no. I'm referring to mankind as a whole" she responded.

"Good, I'm glad, because we must deal with the big picture. Such matters concern all life, and as individuals we are all affected together."

Our Place in the Spheres

The father set the stage for the next discussion with the following: "We should first place ourselves on the Sphere that corresponds to us in this life. In fact, where shall we say we are right now, at what stage?"

"Obviously, we are at the level that includes all the stars and the galaxies" volunteered the youngest.

"Do you both agree with that?" the father inquired, in order to involve the others.

"Yes, of course, rudimentary by now" remarked the sister.

The older brother nodded in agreement.

"All right, we all agree" the father added. "We find ourselves now in Sphere number three. And my reason for identifying it as such is because Sphere number one, as you all recall, was the early conscience of man when he only centered on himself. He dealt with his surroundings in the most fundamental way, as a natural reflex, and spent no effort to contemplate the nature of those surroundings. This doesn't mean he wasn't human; only that he was not experienced in analyzing his environment. Yet, his second stage was soon to come upon him. The need to think things out for his own benefit propelled him into that consciousness. He became confident of himself and of his abilities and relished with appreciation his environment in both its pleasures and its difficulties. He had now become conscious of the earth and thus earth centered. For the longest time he reckoned that his immediate environment was the center of all life around him. By the way, this view of life should not be at all surprising to us, because even to this day this notion persists and is difficult for humans to expel from consciousness! Let's be honest about it.

"A considerable amount of time elapsed and the ability to cope with the environment became ingrained in human consciousness. This, however, did not cause the old basic propensities to disappear from man. Many of his shortcomings remained with him as I just mentioned about earth-centeredness. At the same time, these shortcomings did not prevent man from rising to the next level. So, he began his departure from stage two, the earth consciousness, and embarked on stage three, which is where he is now. The higher his evolution, the quicker his transition becomes to enter the next stage. These are the Gates that he enters and transits as he moves from stage to stage or Sphere to Sphere.

"His consciousness in the third Sphere allows him the awareness of a much greater world around him. But what affects him is not only what he sees and experiences with his natural senses; he is also experiencing a much more intangible transformation in his mind and his consciousness. He now feels the urge to escape the trappings of the physical life. Yes, he is aware of the immensity of the natural universe; yet, despite that and as large as the universe is, it is really not that impossible to measure. Science today speaks of the limits of outer space and the edge of the universe.

"Well? If there is an edge, what's going to happen when we travel to it? Are we going to fall off, the same as once upon a time we would fall off the end of the earth? And if indeed we don't fall off, where will we go?"

"Yes,…really! Where will we go?" questioned our amateur astronomer.

"Indeed, where?" retorted the father. "Then again, why should there be any question: Is there some reason for us to believe that the Creator has failed to provide the means for the continuance of his creation? Ridiculous, wouldn't you say?"

All three youngsters nodded affirmatively.

"Of course, it is ridiculous" he continued. "Now, let's see. The self-centered man did not somehow fall off himself. And later, as earth-centered, he did not fall off the earth either. So, as space-centered, isn't it unlikely that he will fall off the edge of space? And, since his consciousness has expanded so much, we can see where he is able to sense yet another dimension in which he will nestle. Could this then be the life that Jesus committed to man's finding— if man should pursue it for his sake? It can well be. Although, we know nothing about it. For its elevated stature, however, such a life entails a great deal of understanding and wisdom in accepting it and engaging in it. We shall then call it the Sphere of wisdom, and those dwelling therein, wisdom-centered. It is in sequence the Fourth Sphere that is achieved by transiting the Third Gate."

"Since we are cognizant of it, are we to believe that we have entered it?" the youngest questioned.

"We are not to make assumptions of this kind. Suffice it to say that we have come a long way and are at this time competent to sense the existence of yet another dimension of life. It cannot be said whether transiting the Gates at any time happens collectively by all mankind at once or progressively by isolated but increasing numbers of individuals. Nevertheless, it may not be precluded for individuals to sense their own personal experience separate from the aggregate experience."

"I wonder if we could not talk a little about the variance of sensing and knowing. From what you said about adulterating the higher stage with the lower one, I'm thinking if this has not happened here? How is it that the wisdom-stage can be described in our terms when we know nothing about it?" This question came from his daughter.

"Good observation" he admitted. "Although included in your question is your answer. Sensing is itself conveyed to the rational mind by language. That is, our mind forms images about ideas by the use of language. And as we said before, language or words are based on things we know. So, imagery about a fourth Sphere is pictured in our mind by use of language. Therefore, such imagery is adulterated. We are in agreement on that.

"On the other hand, awareness is sensed even though no imagery is involved. Intuition describes this experience best, and it cannot be proved or disproved; except for a possible subsequent outcome that may vindicate or discredit it.

"To cope with our shortcoming, imagery is inevitable in our level of existence. And it is for this reason, as mentioned earlier, that the incarnation of Jesus was necessary. His personage was a medium of communication that satisfied the human need for physical perception—seeing him, hearing him, touching him; and tasting subliminally when he later admonished, as seen in Matthew 26:27-28:

Drink ye all of it; For this is my blood of the new testament …

"And even the charm of fragrance was involved when sweet spices were brought to anoint him, as given by Mark in 16:1.

"For the same reason, the design of the Seven Spheres offers a visual means that triggers a finer intuitive awareness."

His daughter continued in a pensive mood and also eager in her hope for further conversation. She had another question pending: "All right, I can see what you're saying, and I can digest it. There is, however, another subject that's been on my mind, and it seems you touched on it several times in the last things you talked about…"

"Oh,…and what might that be? Have I failed to cover some area?"

"Well, yes. In a way, that's true. The subject was mentioned in *The Great Age* when we all read it; but I hope you will comment on it again now. I'm talking about *time*. It seems you allude to it in most everything you describe; especially, when you refer to developing events and to the past and the future."

"Yes. You're absolutely right. I don't believe there is anything that can be discussed relating to our existence without factoring in the element of time. Our life is time: it is an inexorable ingredient, or multiplier if you will, that combines with various other ingredients to produce a continuum and versatility of life.

"There exists in my view, however, a serious misconception about time. The way I see it, there is *absolute time* and there is *relative time*. Time, which man experiences is relative time; and, although unaware of it, man measures relative time in the context of absolute time.

"We know nothing of absolute time except to sense it or at least to depend upon its existence. We are unable to measure it or to qualify it in any way within the parameters of our current understanding. On the other hand, we have begun to understand relative time, or the time to which we are adapted or of which we are conscious. We have begun to see that it is malleable and that it can be modified as to its *appearance*.

"Relative time can be likened to a piece of elastic or to some *kneadable* material, which in a resting state both have a certain density; but when expanded, they change in appearance. The stretched end may become thinner or even transparent when dragged out enough, while the fixed end may remain dense. The thinness of the stretched end suggests a looser density. And, when this concept of low density is transferred to the notion of time, it may be thought of as a timepiece running...looser and thus faster. This notion, however, is only a simile.

"Science illustrates that a space-traveling clock runs slower than one on earth. Any timepiece traveling faster and farther away will appear slow when calibrated by earth time standards. My view is that space-traveling clocks that run slow or delayed, to the contrary, run faster;...because in their condensed relative-time-delayed function they are registering large portions of absolute time quicker than *normal* time-pieces. In effect, space-traveling clocks are more efficient by shrinking time and space.

"A fitting anecdote is of a person who once asked his friend why he wrote him a sixty-three-page letter. The friend responded it was because he didn't have the time to write a two-page letter!

"All of it paradoxical you might say. Yet, not so: the dual notion of time becomes more evident when time is perceived in reference to the absolute or the unknown of the next higher Sphere.

"In reference to the simile I mentioned, the stretching has only affected the appearance of the elastic material but not its *nature*. Likewise, time appears varied; yet its nature remains intact. Both this planet and one light-year away relate to the same inert frame of reference—fundamental to all other frames. Each planet has its own *relative* perception of the other.

An object observed in *outer space* from earth is itself the *locus where* the earth appears to be in outer space.

"Absolute time is also absolute motion. For man, the absolute is the *unknown*. There, time and motion cease and are for man a concentrated energy whence, you'll recall, the life-creating rays sprang.

"An object moving away from earth at great speed tends to approach and to be converted or transformed into absolute time and absolute motion. However, it is not the object that is traveling *away;* it is, instead, the earth that is *estranged* or distanced from the absolute. Therefore, it is the *nearer-to-absolute* paradoxical high-speed object and not the earth that is the frame of reference or base of observation.

"Man detects relative changes because he is captive within the present structure of relative time. Lest total escape from this Sphere occurs, no discovery can modify man's fundamental consciousness or awareness. Man can dream otherwise, but this is his present reality.

"And, on the subject of falling off the edge of the universe, another notion comes to mind, which I believe you may want to consider. The notion of the universe having an *edge* may be far too presumptuous. That edge may only be a delimitation of our inadequate perception: it may well be that what is considered an edge is but a *horizon*. That is, a horizon outlined in our perception—in some way similar to a three-hundred-and-sixty-degree horizon that we experience when we are in mid-ocean.

"Two possibilities may be considered about our *familiar* universe: One is that we may be *encapsulated* in a balloon-like ever-expanding universe, and because of our limited *view*, we may have a false impression of an authentic edge. On the other hand, our highly touted ever-expanding universe may only be a small area situated *on the surface* of a far greater universe whose size we cannot even imagine. And not only is it the size that we do not know, but also its nature. Again, with our view limited up to the edge of our current universe, we can have no idea what the surface is like on the other side.

"It can be concluded from the above that no precise scientific presumption may be sustained that explains Life and its origin *from the top down*. The only recourse is always to proceed *from the bottom up* in hopes to enrich our knowledge incrementally step by step."

The Sum Up

The father at this point felt that a review of the discussion was needed. He summarized it as follows: "I believe that we must now return to the Master's words and try to sum up the central concept of the discussion we've had.

"When one searches for Life in terms of one's present or known life—regardless of the Sphere level at that time—the ability to know the next level is absent. That is, one remains captive in the current environment. Thus, the admonishment: *He that findeth his life shall lose it.*

"One can find a life of preference only in an environment that is familiar, where comparisons and preferred improvements are available. Meanwhile, the unknown is not yet perceived, which in effect is *lost* to the seeker. When the search, however, is driven for the sake of the *Highest*, the Highest is unveiled; or, in effect *found* at the expense of the lower that in effect is lost. Thus, *He that loseth his life for my sake shall find it.*

"This notion may be stated otherwise: The unknown will be manifested when it is sought in faith and not when pursued in terms of the known. The tools of the known adulterate the search and foreclose on the unknown. It is evident that a positive outcome is not possible for one's own sake, because the seeker is not one's own provider of the unknown. The unknown may only be sought in faith. Thus, the admonishment, *He that loseth his life for my sake shall find it.*"

CHAPTER III

Spheres and Their Limits

Dimensions Described

Bent on his scientific liking for astronomy and joined by his younger brother who enjoyed calculations and numbers, the older son posed this question:

"Of course, we have seen the beautiful art of the Spheres with all the beautiful colors; but is there some basic linear design that supports the art and explains the workings of the concepts you have talked about?"

"Yes, something with numbers that can be worked on?" added the younger brother.

"I believe so, and we should touch on that subject" the father responded. "I will not say that there are numbers involved as such, but there are dimensional values that suggest underlying numbers. The fact is that numbers play no role in understanding the message of the graphic design.

"We must realize that not everyone is interested in referring to a graph; although I believe you are quite justified in bringing up the subject. I say this because in a simple way the graph brings home and clears up an important point made in our discussion. I'm inclined to think that everyone should consider being acquainted with the graph. So, here goes a description:

"All the Spheres we have traversed in the past had their own parameters or limits within which life was engulfed. Human outreach, in other words, cannot exceed the borders within which it is confined. In our current world we consider this our natural environment. It does not matter how extensive that environment may be, because its basic composition remains present throughout, whether near the center or to the farthest extreme."

The older brother asked: "This then is why you said that even if we transfer to some planet in another galaxy, we would soon realize it's quite familiar and that only a variation of the same thing has occurred?"

"That's exactly the way to put it. And this brings us to yet another concept, which in its simplicity will give us a more visual or explicit view of the parameters at work. I don't pretend to say that this method of identifying the parameters is a confirmed method of measurement. However, it is reasonable enough to be accepted as a graphic representation that tends to identify rather than to define."

"Now … what have we got here?" quipped the laconic youngest.

Confines of the Triangles

"Well, let's find out. We can take as a first step the diameter of the earth, which is reported to be 9,926 miles. This number, as I said, does not mean anything with regard to our concept. I mention it only to bring ourselves out of the abstract mindset down to ground level. Now, starting at the center of the diameter—which coincides with the center of the earth—we draw a vertical line straight up until it touches the surface of the earth. This produces three contact points at the earth's surface: which are the one we just mentioned and two more at each end of the diameter. Next, we draw lines to connect all these three points. We have thus drawn a triangle whose base is the diameter and whose two equal sides are the lines we just added. That's it.

"If we keep extending the two lines just drawn and go beyond the point where they meet—that is, at the earth's surface—we will be going away from earth and into space *ad infinitum*. From this simple design, we can now build a dual concept as follows:

"The two extended lines beyond the earth's surface suggest the expansive nature of our own universe. The expansion can go on forever, as the two lines grow farther and farther away from each other and farther and farther into the distance. We should also note that these two lines are not parallel but apart and set in different angles of direction: considering the theory that parallel lines into infinity eventually meet. Furthermore, we should think about the act that in this instance we are associating these details to our physical earth. This means that we have equated the outlying area above the earth's circle to our familiar extraterrestrial space. Another interpretation of the same external area, however, should also be brought to our attention; and we will be touching on this aspect as well.

"The other part of the dual concept mentioned relates to the imaginary triangle we have delineated, which is enclosed within the circumference of the planet. This triangular shape has the misfortune that it cannot be expanded. The fixed size of its base, or diameter of the earth, also sets the height of the triangle; which, in effect, is half the size of the diameter. If per chance the earth should expand or sort of bloat, its diameter would also expand; but all proportions of the sides would remain intact. Therefore, what we perceive is a confined existence that cannot exceed the limits of the earth's fixed dimensions."

"These are all interesting observations. However, how do they tie in with our basic talk ... I mean the strange, the familiar, and all of that?" his daughter asked.

"Yes, yes" he rushed, "you're staying right on top of it. It seems you're always beating me to the punch; but give me time to get there. Remember? We've got to build on things ... one after the other. In fact, I was going there next.

"By the way, ... about the graph: although it can be drawn on paper, we can visualize it in our mind by just describing it with words. Is it OK then with all of you for me to continue?"

The response was a unanimous, "Yes."

"So, ... the triangle we are talking about is a conceptual triangle that corresponds to the confines of the human mind at the level of earth awareness or consciousness—the earth-Sphere. That is, when man was only conscious and limited within himself, that diameter was no wider than his own physical body. When his awareness expanded to encompass his surroundings beyond his physical body, he became conscious of the earth and the distances involved. The breadth of his cognizance increased and grew at the rate of his competence to unveil farther distances. This meant an ever-widening length of the diameter of his consciousness. The more recent indisputable manifestation of this is found very near us in the lingering final stages during the period of Christopher Columbus. We must not deceive ourselves about it...

"And, when he reached the third Sphere and became aware of the universe and its great expanse, that diameter also increased to his perceived outer limits of the universe. In none of the above instances, however, did his consciousness ever exceed the size of the triangle within which it was contained.

"Just think how far man has progressed. In human terms the progress has been dramatic and admirable. Yet, that admiration is in human terms only, and it is limited to what man believes is admirable. Here is where the concept of the triangles comes into play. One can never exceed knowledge that lies within the confines of each triangle, regardless of the triangle's size. The consciousness and knowledge of the second Sphere is indeed broader than that of the first Sphere, but it is never equal to or larger than that of the third Sphere, and so forth.

"It appears reasonable to accept that the higher Sphere always retains the knowledge of the former Sphere. The effect is cumulative, because by logical sequence the awareness that is already attained is foundational to the next higher awareness and is retained. This observation brings us to the outer expansion of the extended sides of the triangle. Here, however, we will be exposed to yet another concept that we will do well to grasp."

"What?...More spheres, more circles?" the youngest quipped.

The Outer Expansion

"The area depicted by the extended sides of the triangle, as I stated, corresponds to the unknown in human consciousness and knowledge. It is the *blank* area I had mentioned earlier. This area

142

is beyond our understanding—since it lies outside the limits of the triangle and thus of the limit of our consciousness, knowledge, or awareness. We may have an intuitive sense of its existence, but we cannot describe it.

"It is an area of much interest to us because it harbors our future in hope and anticipation of improvement and of our greater benefit. It seems that such an expansion can embrace an unlimited amount of space and thus include any number and size of yet to be known spheres up to the sum total of all consciousnesses. For man to reach such levels, it is necessary to traverse future spheres by transiting the Gates one by one. He can only rise to the next level after mastering the previous one. It appears that the achievement of accessing a higher level of consciousness relates much to the acceptance and belief that such exists, which in essence concerns faith.

"Remember what I presented to you as a condition for engaging in this whole discourse. That is, all of what is being presented to you has any significance only if you elect to accept it. For that matter, acceptance does not mean that you condone it. What I am suggesting is that at least you consent to appraise it for its worth and then decide whether to condone it. First, however, you need to accept to listen and to evaluate. You have done this so far; and thus, the way is open for us to embark on some final thoughts.

"The ability to sense intuitive awareness, anticipation, and even an abstract visualization of consciousness higher than that held, requires one's interest and willingness. Such willingness amounts to a burning desire more than a simple alacrity within oneself; that is, a compelling desire to reach and to live at a higher level of life. In the absence of such desire, nothing will happen. This mindset enlarges one's vision of life and one's self-awareness. It requires courage, imagination, and open-mindedness to be able first to accept this and then to achieve it. Once it is reached, however, it forecloses on any likely interest to return to the previous or the lesser state of awareness. An additional effect is to render a new sense of vigor, because of the relative perception of longevity: At age sixty, one feels younger in a span of two hundred years than in one of eighty years. Anxiety is mitigated and hopefulness and enthusiasm increase.

"The artistic rendition of the *Seven Gates to Freedom* forms an inspiring and dependable tool in keeping this vision active, as it can be used at will and for a lifetime. The art's visual representation is swift to contact one's sensitivity and mental receptiveness, making the above concept present and real. The experience is invigorating and reassuring, elevating one's level of confidence, hope, and enthusiasm for life.

"A detached intellectual approach to this will always fail. Acceptance of the Spheres and the sense of assimilating and living through them is required."

Expansion and Linear Design

The father continued: "Our premise, as we said, is that we know nothing about the external area. And the reason is that anything we know is in terms of only what we know within the limitations of the current triangle of consciousness.

"An expansion of our consciousness happens when we transit at the Gate from one Sphere into the next. The Gate is located at the point where the two Spheres touch each other. It could not be otherwise, because if they were not tangent to each other there would be a distance between the Spheres. And a distance between them would mean there would be a chasm of nothingness. When we enter a door into another room, we step out of one room into the next. We don't first fall into an empty space and then climb up into the next room.

"For a graphic representation of what I have described, a linear design has been drawn and is available. If the graph does not convey the message to your satisfaction, it should not be of concern. More important is to grasp the fundamental idea, whether this is by means of a graphic representation, verbal description, or artistic rendition. The most inspiring means, of course, for capturing the message and the sentiment is by viewing the colored illustration of the *Seven Gates to Freedom*. It helps to enjoy the result without reference to technicality. Nevertheless, I will now describe the graph using some of the terms in geometry:

"Two *internally tangent* circles are drawn, and they are *eccentric*— that is, a smaller circle inside a larger one, and perhaps also touching each other at some point in their circumference. In our earlier example we used the earth's diameter to represent the expanse of consciousness at the earth-level. In our present diagram, we will draw circles to mean in abstract form the width of consciousness at any given level. In short, we are repeating the same design without limiting ourselves only to the earth-level consciousness.

"Let's picture in our mind that the highest point in the circumference of the smaller circle is touching the highest point in the circumference of the larger circle. Horizontal diameters are drawn in each circle.

"Likewise, as we had done before, we draw in each circle a vertical line from the center of the diameter to the top where the two circles are tangent. Then, lines are drawn in each circle from the ends of each diameter to the top of the vertical lines where the circles touch. These lines together with the diameter will form *isosceles triangles* inside the respective circles. So, all the lines— which are *chords* of the circles—will intersect at the point where the two circles touch. Regardless of the relative size of the triangles, the area above and outside the circles will coincide. That is the area produced by the extension of the two sides of each triangle and represents the area of the unknown. The symbolism is appropriate, because the unknown is just that: an unknown whose eventual size or any other characteristics we do not know. I am referring to the area formed by the upper *vertical angle* created by the extended sides of each triangle.

"There is also a symbolic description that the larger circle of consciousness embraces all elements of the lesser consciousness in the smaller circle; which means that the lesser consciousness is preserved.

"Here,…I have a copy of the graph, which I think will demonstrate more clearly what I've tried to describe." The father opened a thin folder he had brought and removed a letter-size sheet containing the graph and few explanatory words. He beamed the flashlight on the design for a brief view. He explained how the dark or shaded circle represented the fourth Sphere not yet revealed; and how the white circle symbolized the three Spheres already achieved.

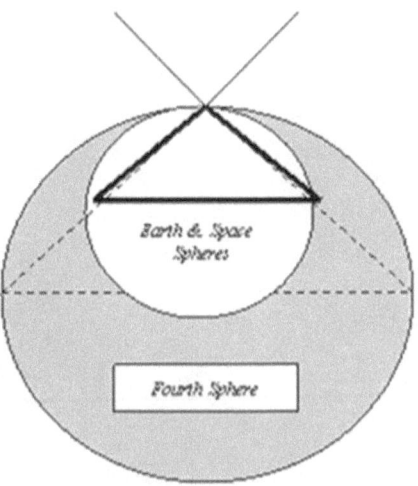

The Unknown
(limitless volume)

The volume of the triangle in the smaller circle means less
<u>awareness</u> *or* <u>consciousness</u> *than of the triangle in the lager circle.*

The area of the angle formed above the circles is the <u>**Unknown**</u>.
It always exceeds the area of any triangle regardless of size.

"Remember" he continued, "all we've talked about is in order to help us focus on the main concept, which is what you would want to digest:

"It is only after we have transferred to the next Sphere through the corresponding Gate, that we become enlightened and informed about that Sphere.

"The prospect of another dimension or dimensions unknown to us in the higher level of consciousness is something that we need to consider as plausible. A higher level of consciousness that encompasses our own consciousness involves more than we are equipped to understand. This may seem distant and speculative to our understanding, short of our actual transition through the Gates to other Spheres. Even in our world, science continues now as it has in the past to debunk its own firm conclusions for lack of adequate advanced knowledge. Our recourse is an open mind and acceptance of possible dramatic and unimaginable variations of what we consider to be the standard of all life. We are destined to be in waiting and in faith until the next season when another of the *Seven Gates to Freedom* shall open; leading us to the Fourth Sphere of awareness of a New Age and onward to the Fifth, Sixth, and Seventh Spheres."

At that point, the youngest raised his hand saying: "There is one thing you have not mentioned at all before, while you spoke about the spiritual part being most important."

"Oh? ... "What is it?"

"Well, you have not mentioned the subject that many people are talking about today, ... the shows on television about extraterrestrial intelligence and all of that. What has this to do in helping us progress to the Spheres?"

"Yes, I didn't make reference. Quite honestly, I believe that to the extent that such help cannot exceed similar help humans offer each other, some exceptional assistance would be forthcoming in the presence of such extraterrestrials.

"I put it this way, because I believe by now the point has been established that anything within our known Sphere of consciousness cannot exceed itself. This includes in my view other possible entities that are also restricted within this very Sphere of consciousness, regardless of their possible super-advanced intelligence. We must remember that under the premise expressed in our discussions, affairs that are of a superior Sphere are not the affairs of the lesser Sphere.

"I will concede that it is possible for such intelligences, if indeed they exist, to be far more advanced in technology, science, and philosophy. Yet, I cannot concede that they are advanced beyond our physical universe. They wouldn't be here if they were.

"And I will venture to go even further. For all we know about them, they may well be most undesirable and quite possibly very dangerous to us. Even at the spiritual level, unknown intercessors who may give the appearance of being helpful are categorically relegated to strict discernment first. Scripture makes a strong point of this in I John 4:1 as follows:

> *Beloved, believe not every spirit, but try the spirits whether they are of God: because many false prophets are gone out into the world.*

"It would be redundant for us to reenter the subject again concerning the importance of self-defense and defensive awareness. It should be clear that our discussion on the subject was related directly to this matter. The provenance of the unclean is an unknown Deviousness and stealth are tools in constant use by such intruders. The only reason to question them about their provenance is to embroil them into confession, but not because of our own simple curiosity. We must remember that our view is on where we are sending them for enlightenment. We are the ones who always look forward in a positive constructive frame of mind.

"You are referring again to the spiritual phase of such encounters" the sister added.

"Of course, I am" the father assured her. "This is the subject of our concern. The physical aspect to a great extent was left outside our purview from the very start of our undertaking. This does not mean that we discount its importance. I believe I have made this very clear several times. That which is of nature is in the hands of science and proper respect must be given. That which is of spirit on the other hand must also be respected."

The older brother, listening to the exchange, now felt compelled to add: "I believe that all of us agree on that point. My question is however, how do we deal with the situation of such possible outside visitors? These days we hear so many reports about such incidents. What should our position be?"

"Again...I believe that such matters belong to the world of science. I mean science in the broadest sense, and that includes the established research systems; academia; government-regulated functions; freelance investigations; the medical, biological, space fields; and all other legitimate and competent interests available."

On the completion of their father's remarks, a long pause ensued. Then, with evident reluctance in voicing his thoughts, the oldest brother again ventured: "I am reserved in saying this; but there is something I need to have cleared up."

"That's fine; ...Just tell me what it is. This is the proper time to resolve your concerns."

"Well, it is similar to sister's question of how can we describe the wisdom-stage or the fourth Sphere in our terms when we know nothing about it...My question is: On what do you even base the existence of higher Spheres when nothing is known about them?..."

The question was unremitting. Its gist and pragmatism were impregnable, the whole effort had been to induce another approach to wisdom and to encourage an alternative view of life. But now,...what? Was the whole task a waste?

In a calm and reassuring voice, the father responded, "I cannot but praise you on your question. I believe that in concluding our discussions, a more fitting question could not have been raised. The response I will give you, however, is the one I have already given. You will all recall that at the start of our discourse months ago I was questioned about the source of my information. My answer was that part of it I had read and otherwise the rest was intuitive knowledge; ...and I will leave it at that.

"It is the combined understanding of the present and the future that I have tried to impart to you on condition that you may or may not accept it. My hope is that you will want to extract from it the most advantage. Beyond this, I will only add that if one seeks to expand into the realm of the soul, it is folly to reduce the effort to the level of wormholes, time warps, spatial searches, and hopes of salvation by presumed superior intelligences. Such, only enrich and vary the physical state of man through novel and fascinating natural experiences and discoveries, but not beyond; for they are all events confined within the present limits of consciousness. It is wasteful of life's precious treasure to be engaged in futility."

The Art and the Message

How to View the Seven Gates to Freedom

One final but important step remained in the father's mind. He needed to explain about the artwork as an indispensable tool in understanding and enjoying the notion of the rise to the Spheres.

"There is a direct relationship between what we have discussed and the colorful art of the *Seven Gates to Freedom*. You are now aware that the message conveyed in our talks is the same as that conveyed by the art.

"As may be expected, the art offers a living experience of connection with the Spheres—depending on one's imagination and concentration. A real sensation of transiting the Gates can be felt. The content of the art is captivating and soothing and produces an instant willingness to be absorbed into the cosmic ambiance that it displays.

"Whether the verbal description or the art should come first is a matter of preference. Each of the approaches stands alone. Together, however, they heighten the effect: The verbal approach provides description; the artistic approach provides the sentiment.

"The art is best displayed in full lighting. The Spheres should be discerned and contemplated by the viewer. Concerns and preoccupations should be suspended, as the moment is for rising.

The viewer should transfer to the scene displayed in the art and identify with the image in two ways:

"One is to look outward through the Spheres from the vantage point of the human figure on the earth. The other is to reverse the approach and look inward toward the human figure from the vantage point of the outer golden Sphere. The net effect is that in the first approach the viewer has the sensation of looking outward into an expanding universe. The second approach gives the feeling that one is immersed in the highest Sphere looking down through layers of Spheres at the human figure standing on the earth's surface. In all, the experience is total and absorbing when one applies oneself and projects oneself. It is always invigorating and can be repeated as often as one may wish. Awareness of this type has a positive and edifying effect on the individual. It promotes an optimistic attitude and an agreeable disposition; broadens the view of life; eases anxiety and tension; rejuvenates; and enriches the estimation of one's own self in knowing where the next step is.

"It is my hope that everything we have discussed will be of most benefit to you and to all those people in your life who may come in contact with you.

The worldly is not Divine. And the Divine is not worldly.

Then saith he unto them, … Render therefore unto
Caesar the things which are Caesar's; and unto God the
things that are God's. (Mat. 22:21).

APPENDIX

Reference Notation

Following is an Abstract for a paper that appeared in the proceedings of the May 1995 Abisko meeting on "Limits to Scientific Knowledge", titled *Boundaries and Barriers,* eds. J. Casti and A. Karlqvist (Reading, MA: Addison-Wesley), 1996, pp. 148-187.

Author: **Piet Hut**, School of Natural Sciences Institute for Advanced Study Princeton, NJ 08540.

Structuring Reality: The Role of Limits

The paradox of limits lies in the fact that limits combine two opposite functions: setting apart and joining. They partition the world (in fact, all that appears in any form) into separate areas, in intricate and overlapping hierarchies. But at the same time, they structure the interrelationships and communication channels between the pieces into which they seem to have carved up the world.

We can view the world of appearance as an intricate interplay of limits, each acting within their own realm of validity. However, this limiting role is *only* a role. For each context, we can find a wider context, within which the limitation implied in the narrower context loses its sting, so to speak. As a consequence, the most basic structure of the world is the notion of role, of 'as'. This view denies the existence of ultimate limits to knowledge, scientific or otherwise, suggesting a radical optimism, in the form of a freedom from identification.

Source:

http://www.swif.uniba.it/lei/mind/topics/00000032.htm#Naturalizing%20phenomenology

Bibliography

Cognitivist vs. Nativist Theories —
[*Concerning human adaptation to language.*]

Cowie, Fiona. *What's Within?: Nativism Reconsidered.* New York, Oxford University Press, 1999.

Rogoff, Barbara. *Apprenticeship in Thinking: Cognitive Development in Social Context.* New York, Oxford University Press, 1990.

Tomasello, Michael and Bates, Elizabeth. *Language Development: The Essential Readings (Essential Readings in Developmental Psychology).* Malden, MA, Blackwell Publishers Inc., Nov. 2001.

Intuitionism —
[*Its contributing role vis-à-vis the perception of ... realities.*]

Church, Alonzo. *Introduction to Mathematical Logic.* Princeton, N.J., Princeton University Press, 1996.

Mermin, N. David. *It's About Time: Understanding Einstein's Relativity.* Princeton, NJ, Princeton University Press, 2005.

Steiner, Miriam. "The Search for Order in a Disorderly World: Worldviews and Prescriptive Decision Paradigms."

International Organization Vol. 37, No. 3 (Summer, 1983), pp. 373-413   JSTOR.[Online].   http://links.jstor.org/sici?sici= 0020-8183(198322)37%3A3%3C373%3ATSFOIA%3E2.0. CO%3B2-Z

Van Dalen, Dirk. *Mystic, Geometer, and Intuitionist: The Life of L. E. Brouwer.* New York, Oxford University Press, 1999.

Views on Cosmology —
[*The presumption always of a ...physical start—a* "point."]

Gurth, Alan H. and Steinhardt, Paul J. "The Inflationary Universe." *The World of Physics: A Small Library of the Literature of Physics from Antiquity to the Present* by Jefferson Hane Weaver. New York, Simon and Schuster, 1987, U.8, pp. 318-319.

"Inflationary Universe Cosmology." *McGraw-Hill Encyclopedia of Science and Technology.* 10th ed. New York, McGraw Hill, 2007. v. 9, pp. 149-156.

Index

To identify subject areas, relate
CONTENTS and INDEX
page numbers

Seven Gates to Freedom

Home/Latest Reviews, Religion, Self-Improvement/Seven Gates to Freedom

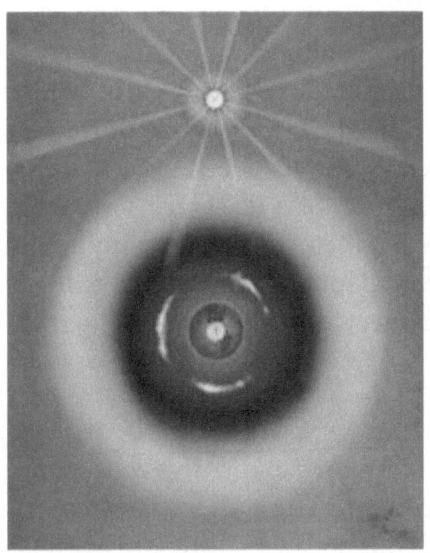

Seven Gates to Freedom

Title: Seven Gates to Freedom: Awareness and Consciousness
Author: Ayla Hesperia and Dr. Mark Athanasios C. Karras
Publisher: New-Byzantium.org
ISBN: 979-8892160001
Pages: 188
Genre: Cosmology / Self-Help / Religion & Spirituality
Reviewed by: Jack Chamber

Hollywood Book Reviews

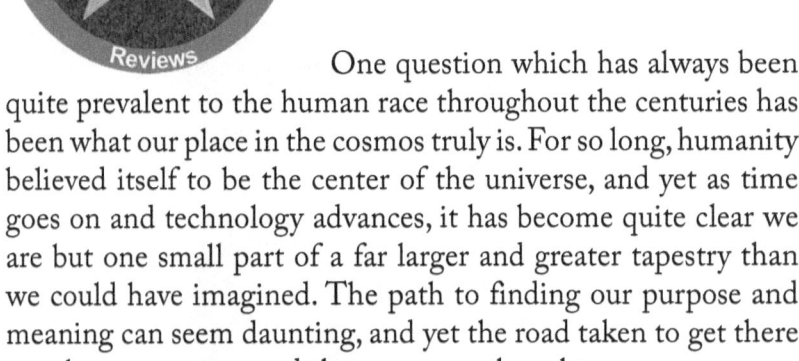

One question which has always been quite prevalent to the human race throughout the centuries has been what our place in the cosmos truly is. For so long, humanity believed itself to be the center of the universe, and yet as time goes on and technology advances, it has become quite clear we are but one small part of a far larger and greater tapestry than we could have imagined. The path to finding our purpose and meaning can seem daunting, and yet the road taken to get there may be more connected than we once thought.

In authors Ayla Hesperia (Pseudonym) and Dr. Mark Athanasios C. Karras's *Seven Gates to Freedom: Awareness and Consciousness*, the author explores this concept through a blend of science and spirituality. The author shares a means of connecting to the greater consciousness through an understanding and communion with our own awareness, allowing the reader over time to gain a far wider perception of life and the universe as a whole. The book uses illustration and spirituality to connect to the reader, and yet finds the reader exploring concepts of spheres of human understanding and awareness, redefining the purpose behind the multiverse theory.

The author does a marvelous job of finding the perfect balance between narrative storytelling from a non-fiction standpoint, guided practices to use this technique themselves, and educational value. What stood out to me immediately was the authors' ability to showcase their experiences and thought-processes without turning the book into a sermon of sorts, allowing both religious and non-religious readers to approach the topic from their own perspectives.

This allowed for a more fluid and memorable reading experience, amplifying the imagery and voice the authors found in their writing style to speak for itself. The way the author was able to relay the connection between the mind, spirit, and body was remarkable to read, and those connections being part of the greater cosmos is something which has always resonated with me personally.

This is the perfect read for those who enjoy non-fiction reads, especially those who enjoy cosmology, spiritualism, religious reads, and personal transformation stories and guides. The exploration of energy sources and outputs allowed both the scientific minded and spiritually driven alike to connect to the source material, and the way the author presents these findings through the explanation to his children allows the readers to feel a more personal tone and connection. Religious readers will appreciate the chapters dedicated to the concept of faith and God's role in the author's discoveries, and yet the respect and openness in which the author writes allows so many other readers to feel included or intrigued enough to really get lost in the author's lessons.

Memorable, engaging, and thoughtful, authors Ayla Hesperia and Dr. Mark Athanasios C. Karras's *Seven Gates to Freedom: Awareness and Consciousness* is a must-read non-fiction book on spirituality, personal transformation, and cosmology. The knowledge and almost philosophical approach to the subject the author takes allows the readers to deeply think through the ideas being presented to them, and gives a feeling of openness and discussion all books in this genre should always approach from.

Pacific Book Review

helping authors succeed!

Title: Seven Gates to Freedom: Awareness and Consciousness
Authors: Ayla Hesperia and Dr. Mark Athanasios C. Karras
Publisher: New-Byzantium
ISBN: 979-8892160001
Pages: 188
Genre: Cosmology / Self-Help / Religion & Spirituality
Reviewed by: Dan MacIntosh

Pacific Book Review

Seven Gates to Freedom: Awareness and Comsciousness, written under the Pseudonym Ayla Hesperia, is a unique and unusual book. It's part religious, part self-help, and is intellectually deep. Reading it is, to put it mildly, an experience.

It's also a book within a book, so to speak. It begins with a father explaining some deep philosophial concepts to his three children. These conversations are the best parts of the book because they tale difficult-to-comprehend concepts and put them into an easier to understand format. This form of exploring heavy concepts is not new, by the way. Plato also wrote in dialogues, as well, so Hesperia has learned some of his methods from the best minds.

What makes it into a book within a book, is how the father asks these children to read *The Great Age* (a section included within this book) and then discuss its contents. You may feel a little bit like these younger ones while reading this inner work, however.

Although it contains some resonating ideas, it's also packed with stream of consciousness ideas that are lengthy and may be difficult to fully digest for the average Reader.

This is not a book about Christianity, although New Testament Scriptures are quoted throughout. Nevertheless, the author states, when desciding the work, "The message conveyed is the true message of Jesus. It is there that he is found. Religious affiliation is not a requirement for reaping the benefit." Such thinking sure sounds a lot like a 'spiritual, but not religious' approach to understanding God. This may be an incorrect assesment, but at least reads this way.

Another unique factor in the presentation of this written work is the cover's illustration. The back of the book explains: "The integrity of the art on the front cover must not be compromised. It is in pure form and free of any written words or distractions. Experience the message in the illustration. The book will assist and, if the approach intrigues you, there is good reason. Meet the challenge offered by the illustration and the book. Their message is simple and direct, encouraging youthfulness while aging.

Attempting to describe the cover art isn't easy. In short, though, it has a kind of sci-fi feel to it, showing a tiny human surrounded by circular illustrations of a vast universe around him. The author suggests readers "experience the message in the llustration." This reader can't say he experienced this message, but your connection to the words and art may be better and more memorable.

At book's end, Hesperia writes: "As may be expected, the art offers a living experience of connection with the Spheres— depending on one's imagination and concentration. A real sensation of transiting the Gates can be felt. The content of the art is captivating and soothing and produces an instant willingness to be absorbed into the cosmic ambiance that it displays." Hopefully, you have the kind of transformative experience Hesperia details in this postscript.

Certainly, this is not any sort of typical spiritual/religious work. It's an extensive, detailed book, filled with fully thought-out ideas. It's also a unique combination of the editorial and artistic, due to its significant cover art. There are a multitude of possible reactions to reading this book, depending upon where the reader is at, spiritually. For those open to completely ingesting the various ideas put forth, it has the potential to be lifechanging. Alternately, those that come to the book with sort of a casual attitude about reading it, may be a little overwhelmed by how it delves so deeply into philosophical thought. Ayla Hesperia has put all the work into it, though, so the rest is all up to you and your unique attitude toward the book.

ISBN 9798892160001
All Rights Reserved.
Published in the United States of America
Printed by Creative Books Highlands Square, Pittsburg, CA.
Copyright 2021 by Mark Athanasios C. Karras